Second Edition

ST. LOUIS PARKS

Reedy Press
PO Box 5131
St. Louis, MO 63139, USA

Library of Congress Control Number: 2024948780

ISBN: 9781681065885

Please visit our website at www.reedypress.com.

Design by Rich Roden and Linda Eckels

Printed in Canada
25 26 27 28 29   5 4 3 2 1

Second Edition

ST. LOUIS PARKS

NINI HARRIS AND ESLEY HAMILTON

Photography by Mark Scott Abeln,
Steve Tiemann, Mark Groth, and NiNi Harris

REEDY PRESS

Courtesy of Mark Groth

CONTENTS

Phlox at Greensfelder Park
Courtesy of Steve Tiemann

Willmore Park
Courtesy of Mark Groth

Courtesy of Mark Abeln

ACKNOWLEDGMENTS

St. Louis Public Library staff members, including Adele Heagney with the St. Louis Room; Louise Powderly and Cynthia Millar, formerly of the History and Genealogy Departments, Main Branch; Steve Kozlowski with the Carpenter Branch; and Cynthia E. Jones, retired manager of the Carpenter Branch, helped locate documents and historical data concerning the development of the St. Louis City Parks and Recreation Department and of individual city parks. Their help was invaluable.

Lesley Hoffarth, president and executive director of Forest Park Forever, and Carey Bundy, formerly with Great Rivers Greenway, provided data concerning the number and variety of trees in specific parks and usage of local parks. The late Mary Ann Simon and the late Lois Waninger of Carondelet Historical Society helped locate first-person accounts recalling parks in the Carondelet area. Daniel W. Skillman, former commissioner of parks, made historical materials available to the author. Sue Clancy, executive director of Forest Park Forever, 1993–1998, recounted the evolution of the master plan for Forest Park and the Restoring the Glory campaign. Dan McGuire, alderman of the 28th Ward, 1981–1997, and director of Parks, Recreation, and Forestry, 1997–2001, shared his dedication to the parks and his knowledge of their history.

For additions and updates to this second edition of *St. Louis Parks*, Adele Heagney and Kirwin Roach of the St. Louis Room, Main Branch of the St. Louis Public Library, assisted with finding historical documentation of state parks. Pamela Daugherty of Forest Park Forever updated information about that park's incredible tree census. Joseph Hart, forestry supervisor for Tower Grove Park, provided current information concerning Tower Grove's impressive variety of trees.

Volunteers Sharon Roberts and Brian Kolde assisted with collecting historical materials concerning the Missouri state parks. Kayla Dunn with the Friends of Carondelet Park gave input about the impressive, volunteer-fueled projects in Carondelet Park.

PREFACE

Francis Park
Courtesy of Mark Abeln

Reedy Press published the first edition of *St. Louis Parks* in 2012. My friend Esley Hamilton, an authority on St. Louis County history, wrote the chapters on the county parks—an expansive system developed in the latter half of the 20th century. As a St. Louis City historian, I had the honor of writing about the evolution of the city parks, which feature Victorian and early 20th-century landscapes that are integral to the design and life of their neighborhoods.

In recent decades, the expansion of the metropolitan area has encroached on surrounding natural areas. Simultaneously, St. Louisans have helped ring the metro area with rugged state parks and conservation areas. These parks and areas that preserve natural terrains are critical for the environment, for maintaining natural habitats and for the quality of life of St. Louisans. I have chronicled their establishment with additional chapters for this second edition of *St. Louis Parks*.

These new chapters follow the story of the park movement in St. Louis from the creation of the first park west of the Mississippi, Lafayette Park, to the creation of Confluence Point State Park in the new millennium.

—NiNi Harris

Lafayette Park duck house
Courtesy of Mark Abeln

PROLOGUE

Bee Tree Park
Courtesy of Steve Tiemann

O'Fallon Park
Courtesy of NiNi Harris

When my great-great-grandfather settled in South St. Louis in 1864, the first job he got was planting trees in a city park. At that time, St. Louisans were nursing wounded soldiers convalescing in makeshift hospitals across St. Louis. The city was absorbing waves of refugees from the Civil War, including many Blacks recently freed from slavery. A Confederate Army still threatened St. Louis in a last-ditch effort to turn the Civil War in their favor.

While St. Louis was facing this most dire circumstance of its history, the leadership and citizens demonstrated their commitment to establishing a park system that would bring joy to the entire community for generations. They maintained parks that had been created when St. Louis was still a frontier boomtown—Lafayette Park in 1836, Lucas Park in 1857, and Hyde Park in 1854. These parks were already the centerpieces of their neighborhoods. Also during this terrifying era, civic leaders discussed creating more, much larger parks. They had a vision of parks lush with trees, filled with birdsong, fountains, and delightful pavilions.

Thanks to the foundation laid by civic leaders during the mid-19th century, public parks became a focus of St. Louis life for the next century and a half. St. Louis philanthropists and taxpayers supported establishing Tower Grove Park, sprawling Forest Park, expansive O'Fallon Park on the North Side and Carondelet Park on the South Side. As the decades passed, the city's network of parks grew to number a hundred ranging from pocket parks to 1,300-acre Forest Park. Uses grew to include activities and sports. As children, major league baseball players Joe Garagiola and Yogi Berra and world-class soccer players from The Hill and from the Spanish community in Carondelet honed their skills playing on the fields in St. Louis city parks.

As development spilled over the city limits, St. Louis County established the county parks system in 1951 that now includes nearly 12,000 acres. Beginning with the donation of pristine forests and glades in 1934 for Babler State Park, St. Louisans spurred the creation of Missouri State Parks to ring St. Louis with natural, rugged landscapes. The Missouri Department of Conservation maintains reserves around St. Louis that purify

Creve Coeur Lake
Courtesy of Steve Tiemann

and sweeten the air and provide habitat for wildlife.

As our civic ancestors envisioned, the parks—city parks, county parks, Missouri state parks and reserves—enrich our lives. My husband and I walk in a city park three or four times a week. While enjoying the natural settings we see people bird-watching, biking trails, listening to concerts, gazing at the stars through telescopes, and enjoying camaraderie at a beer garden.

The activities have evolved and changed through the decades, but the joy taken in these shared public spaces remains constant.

On a summer afternoon years ago, I saw a young couple sitting on a picnic blanket sipping wine amid the tall grasses around the lily ponds in Tower Grove Park. Nearby, an 8-year-old girl ran around the ponds. The girl, on a field trip, was from a troubled family. That day, she watched the ducks, dozens of them, gracefully floating on the lake. Then they clumsily waddled across the nearby lawns toward her. She ran to them and they took flight rising above her. Excited by the ducks flying over her head, she threw her arms up in the air and shouted, "I can't believe this is happening to me!"

—NiNi Harris

Bandstand, Tower Grove Park
Courtesy of Mark Abeln

Pagoda Island, Forest Park
Courtesy of Mark Abeln

CITY PARKS

NiNi Harris

The definition of St. Louis city parks includes picturesque squares with lush greenery, towering sycamores framing ball fields, and expansive, rolling landscapes with cascading fountains and shimmering lakes. The city boasts more than 100 parks that cover 3,250 acres and are as varied as its neighborhoods. The number and scale of the parks result from the commitment of generations of St. Louisans. This commitment to common spaces dates from when St. Louis was a French village through the ongoing restoration of Forest Park.

Public parks were the stepchild of the Industrial Revolution. Factories meant concentrated jobs, which meant more people, which meant much larger cities. The need for public gardens, yards, and spaces grew with the size of cities—in Europe and America. Young St. Louis, the gateway to a rugged frontier, was a leader in creating parks.

This remarkable park system began with St. Louis's origin as a French fur trading post in the wilderness. Our French founders surveyed common fields for farming. Within these common fields, villagers were awarded strips of land to cultivate. The villagers worked together to fence the periphery of the common fields. The founders also set aside land as commons—land jointly owned by the villagers and used for grazing or gathering firewood. This system of community ownership and improvement for the common good was similar in concept to 19th- and 20th-century parks.

In 1836, Mayor John Darby scouted wilds far beyond the city limits for a parade ground and park, later named Lafayette Park. The acreage of Lafayette Park, like a number of early parks, was set aside from the old French commons for public use. These common-land parks are often said to date to 1812, the year the United States government recognized St. Louis's ownership of the old village's commons.

Some early parks were donated—Jackson Place in 1816, Carr Square in 1844, and St. Louis Place in 1850. The city purchased the land for Hyde Park in 1854 and transformed an old cemetery to create Benton Park in 1866. By the end of the Civil War, the city owned 287 acres of parks, places, and squares. Then one citizen with a vision for

Courtesy of Mark Abeln

The 1904 World's Fair was constructed over the western half of Forest Park.
Courtesy of the Library of Congress

public parks doubled the size of the system. English-born St. Louisan Henry Shaw donated land for Tower Grove Park and then guided its elegant development.

Citizens and civic leaders debated the advantages of large parks versus small neighborhood parks or squares. Ultimately, St. Louisans established both.

Coinciding with the separation of the city from the county in 1876, the city established three expansive parks on its periphery—179-acre Carondelet Park in far South City, now 127-acre O'Fallon Park in far North City, and one of the largest urban parks in the nation, now 1,293-acre Forest Park.

Unlike the earlier pedestrian parks, Tower Grove, Carondelet, O'Fallon, and Forest Parks were destinations for carriage drives. These parks on the outskirts of the city were at first criticized as available only for the well-to-do, distant from working-class neighborhoods. The wisdom of establishing these parks gradually became apparent as they spurred well-planned, handsome residential developments and as mass transit made them accessible to the entire community.

The City Water Division also established two parks in the late 19th century. These parks—Reservoir and Chain of Rocks—were created to provide a purified setting, with trees filtering the air around the then-open reservoirs.

Large or small, the city's parks were sylvan retreats that often boasted lush gardens and lakes. These were places for pleasant strolls, carriage rides, picnics, boating, and delightful resorts for St. Louisans to join thousands of their neighbors for the popular summer band concerts.

St. Louisans expanded their definition of public parks

"The parks are not only for the birds and worms, but primarily for men, women, and children, and not only for optical delight, but especially for use for health, happiness, and the fostering of a lively public spirit."
—Mayor Rolla Wells

Tower Grove Park
Courtesy of the Library of Congress

during the first decade of the 20th century. Civic leaders recognized that parks could increase the health and happiness of the entire citizenship and physically tie together the disparate city neighborhoods with efficiency and beauty. They developed two major plans that would guide the system's growth for decades—the small park and playground program and the boulevard system.

Small parks were designed to address the shortage of park acreage near downtown and along the river, where most St. Louisans lived. The Civic Plan published in 1907 documented the comparative shortage of park space in this crowded eastern part of the city. While there was one acre of park area to every 97 persons living between Grand Boulevard and the city limits—and there was one acre of park area to every 701 persons living between Grand and Jefferson—between Jefferson Avenue and the river, there was only one acre of park area to every 1,871 persons.

The distinctive fountain that once graced Hyde Park
Courtesy of NiNi Harris

Beginning in 1903, the city began creating pocket parks and playgrounds in the crowded neighborhoods near downtown, along the river, and in its industrial corridor. The city adopted the program of organized play that two local groups—the Wednesday Club and Civic Improvement League—had tested. A new commission for playgrounds and recreation hired social reformer Charlotte Rumbold as secretary or superintendent of the program. The immediate popularity of the playground program evidenced its importance. Playground attendance during the summer school vacation of 1908 averaged 6,798 each day. Attendance at the playgrounds for the school year ending in April 1909 totaled 471,941. The daily cost per child was 1.9 cents. Rolla Wells, who served as mayor from 1901 to 1909, stated that the playground program "was admired and emulated by other cities, and, I think, became the standard of organized public play for the whole nation."

As a consultant to the St. Louis parks, the great landscape architect George Kessler proposed a boulevard system designed to create an emerald necklace of parks and boulevards. In 1907, he proposed ringing St. Louis and connecting its neighborhoods with parks and greenery.

German-born Kessler had emigrated to the United States as a child. He returned to Germany to study landscape gardening and civil engineering. Kessler began his career in Kansas City and is credited with that city's park and boulevard system.

The challenge facing Kessler was that the city lies in the shape of an ellipse between the Mississippi and the city limits. The early roads reached out from downtown like spokes on a wheel. Kessler proposed the Kingshighway Boulevard Plan, which followed and extended Kingshighway. The plan connected existing parks, added new parks, and crossed and connected all the spokes or major roads.

Kingshighway was improved and straightened and viaducts were built over railbeds. With its extensions, Kingshighway Boulevard linked Carondelet Park, Tower Grove Park, Forest Park, and the 19th-century cemeteries adjacent to O'Fallon

Park (Bellefontaine and Calvary) on the north side. Bellerive, Christy, and Penrose Parks were added along the boulevard system. Parkways in the center of North Kingshighway, and the southeastern extensions of Kingshighway, later renamed Bellerive and Holly Hills Boulevards, enhanced the system.

At the same time, Kessler guided the reconstruction of Forest Park after the 1904 World's Fair. Cass Gilbert, architect of the US Supreme Court Building, the Saint Louis Art Museum, and St. Louis Public Library's magnificent Central Library, designed the reconstruction of Forest Park's grand basin.

St. Louisan Dwight F. Davis, national tennis doubles champion from 1899 to 1901 and namesake of the Davis Cup in tennis, became commissioner of St. Louis Parks in 1911. Politically a Teddy Roosevelt–style Progressive, this wealthy St. Louisan believed in organized recreation to promote health, happiness, and build character in all St. Louisans. Davis added tennis courts, golf courses, swimming pools, and ball fields to pastoral retreats with the notion that the city's parks should be utilized to their fullest extent rather than being merely admired.

The resulting system—with expansive parks and small neighborhood parks, formal gardens and natural landscapes, abundant trees that filtered and sweetened the air, sun-showered meadows or fields, and plentiful athletic fields for endless hours of fun—served the entire citizenship throughout the 20th century. That century put extra demands on the park system, and a new commitment to public parks was necessary. A monumental bond issue in 1923 funded a ribbon of parkway downtown, new neighborhood parks, and improvements to existing parks.

The House of Refuge stood on the site of current-day Marquette Park. *Courtesy of NiNi Harris*

The hardships of the Depression and World War II increased the use of park facilities while resources and manpower were most limited. From 1931 to 1934, the number of large picnics requiring permits increased from 285 to 500. In the summer of 1934, attendance in organized playground programs surpassed 1 million children. The federally sponsored works programs designed to combat unemployment helped the city address its own shrinking budget to maintain parks during the Great Depression. It also added a new dimension to the parks' landscapes—Works Progress Administration stonework.

Laborers with the WPA crafted their distinctive stonework in parks across the city. They built stone walks and steps that looked as if they were from a land of enchantment. They built white limestone barbeque pits that instantly became landmark features. In small playgrounds, they crafted stone retaining walls that were much more than decorative. The stone walls stopped erosion and added square footage to the valuable play areas.

During World War II, the United States Army built a 17-acre recreation camp in the southeastern corner of Forest Park. The camp could accommodate 1,500 soldiers. The families of young men fighting the battles of World War II found healthful recreation, distraction, and peace in the city parks.

St. Louisans demonstrated both vision and optimism in 1944—while war still raged in Europe and in the Pacific; while meat, tires, gasoline, and other staples were rationed; and while many of their sons, brothers, and husbands were in harm's way. In this trying and frightening environment, they passed a bond issue to ensure that the parks could be equipped for future generations.

Following the war, baby boomers packed the parks. The postwar building boom filled in the empty lots and edges of the city with more houses and more families. Willmore, Tilles, and Lindenwood Parks were developed and dedicated to serve families in these booming neighborhoods of Southwest City. The city acquired the 13.2-acre site of Barrett Brothers Park in the Arlington neighborhood. In 1962, the city developed the Dwight F. Davis Park (now known as Gregory J. Carter Park) in the Walnut Park neighborhood.

In recent decades, while the city's population shrank, and while St. Louis faced the challenges that all major American cities have faced, the citizens have repeatedly expressed their love for their parks. In 1993, city voters passed a half-cent sales tax partly to fund and upgrade their parks. In 2000, they passed Proposition C, which created the Metropolitan Parks and Recreation District now known as the Great Rivers Greenway. This new dedicated funding enabled the city to work with surrounding counties to preserve natural lands, restore and improve existing parks, and create a new network of trails uniting and enhancing its parks.

While citizens supported their parks, the common spaces were acting as keystones in the rebirth of historic neighborhoods. Lafayette and Benton Parks added to the Victorian charm of their historic neighborhoods. In other neighborhoods, proximity to Clifton Heights, Carondelet, and Francis Parks kept property values high. Beginning in the 1990s, the parks' new state-of-the-art playgrounds attracted young families.

Citizens helped develop master plans for Carondelet, Forest, Francis, Hyde, and Lafayette Parks. The creation of Citygarden in the heart of downtown and the spectacular, ongoing restorations of Tower Grove and Forest Parks reflect the same commitment to the common good that guided the development of the remarkable city park system during the 19th and 20th centuries.

While the comprehensive St. Louis city park system serves all neighborhoods in the city, it also can claim two of the nation's outstanding parks. Thanks to massive private donations supplementing tax support, Tower Grove Park ranks as the finest Victorian Park in the nation and Forest Park is praised as the nation's stellar urban park.

Founded	Size	Cost
1836	30 Acres	Reserved from common fields

LAFAYETTE PARK

Courtesy of Mark Groth

Courtesy of NiNi Harris

Framed by an ornate iron fence topped with fleur-de-lis finials, lush Lafayette Park is the oldest park west of the Mississippi. Created during the Victorian era, the park boasts an enchanting 19th-century landscape that is the focal point of its Victorian Lafayette Square neighborhood.

In 1836, St. Louis Mayor John F. Darby reserved the 30-acre square from the sale of the old St. Louis commons for the park. He described the site as it originally appeared. It was “covered with underbrush of young hickory and oak bushes, and in some places with patches of hazel and sumac bushes. The view of the city, in the distance, from these beautiful grounds was at the time charming indeed.”

In 1868, the park was embellished by a statue of Senator Thomas Hart Benton by sculptor Harriet Hosmer. Its unveiling was witnessed by a crowd of 40,000. A year later, a bronze copy of Jean-Antoine Houdon’s statue of George Washington was dedicated in the park.

A city ordinance officially established the park and named it for General Lafayette in 1851. Citizens moving to its vicinity contributed to its improvements. At the beginning of the Civil War, however, the park was used as a military camp. “Beautiful Lafayette Park, with its brilliant flower beds and stretches of green sward, looking like emerald velvet, was turned into a great military camp,” St. Louisan Sarah Hill recalled the park in 1861. “Regiments from adjacent states were sent here for organization and drill . . . now campfires were burning. . . . Tents were erected and laid out in streets. It was hot, dry, and dusty, and clouds of dust blew and added to the general discomfort.”

Courtesy of Mark Abeln

Courtesy of Mark Abeln

Courtesy of Mark Abeln

City financing of park improvements began in 1864. European-trained landscape architect Maximillian G. Kern guided the development of the park. He designed a fantasyland of curious plants, creepers, mosses, beautiful foliage, grottoes, shady nooks, and glades. In 1888, *Commercial and Architectural St. Louis* claimed that Lafayette Park was "one of the handsomest pieces of landscape architecture to be found in the United States."

The most deadly tornado in St. Louis history swept through this idyllic landscape on May 27, 1896. It ripped the mighty shade trees from their roots. It was decades before giant tulip trees, willows, black pines, and elms again shaded the park. In 1927, the *St. Louis Star* described the restored park, "there are quaint by-paths and curious rock work, and shimmering pools in leafy dells waiting to be explored."

The *Star* editorialized against a new threat to the park: "Don't Despoil Lafayette Park," decrying the proposal to use it as an "air landing field" to serve nearby downtown. Then World War II posed threats with proposals to scrap the park's fence for the metal drive to build tanks. Following the war, and mirroring the neighborhood, the park suffered from deferred maintenance.

Beginning in 1968, as more and more new residents started renovating the 19-century townhouses and mansions surrounding the park, they also began restoring the park's whimsy and charm. Step by step, they revived the damaged finials on the fence, planted an iris garden, and refreshed the Second Empire–style police station. The park became home to the Vintage Baseball Association. Residents worked with city officials to develop a master plan to guide further enhancements to Lafayette Park.

Lafayette Park gates at night in the snow
Courtesy of Mark Abeln

Courtesy of Mark Abeln

Founded	Size	Cost
1866	14.3 Acres	Former City Cemetery

BENTON PARK

Courtesy of Mark Abeln

A Victorian pleasure ground, Benton Park spurred the 19th-century development of its neighborhood and the restoration of its then-historic neighborhood at the turn of the millennium. The park began as the City Cemetery on the road leading to the federal arsenal. When the cemetery was established in 1833, it was far beyond the city's boundaries. Due to the growth and expansion of St. Louis, the graves were moved with reburial at the quarantine section of Arsenal Island in 1856. The year following the Civil War, the city dedicated the old cemetery as a park in the new, developing South City area. The park was named for Missouri's first senator and proponent of manifest destiny, Thomas Hart Benton.

As park keeper, German immigrant and horticulturist Edward Krausnick transformed the abandoned cemetery into a luxuriant 14.3-acre park. The city financed his efforts, spending almost $93,000 on Benton Park during the Gilded Age. As the red-brick German neighborhood grew around the park, the park itself became "confessedly one of the most beautiful attractions of the City," according to *Commercial and Architectural St. Louis.*

Reflecting the German character of the new neighborhood in 1882, citizens dedicated a granite obelisk in Benton Park honoring German-American Colonel Friedrich Hecker. This patriot raised a regiment of local German-Americans during the Civil War, serving first under General John C. Frémont and later commanding his own brigade in the Union Army. A Germanic St. Louisan, architect Ernest C. Janssen, designed the shaft of the monument.

During the 1890s, South St. Louisans flocked to the park for the summer concerts held on Saturday nights. The evolution of the surrounding urban neighborhood and of the cemetery into an urban resort was clear in the description in the Parks's annual report of 1900. "The park, although in the midst of a thickly built-up part of the city, is a delightful retreat. The ground is naturally very broken, and with its two lakes, grotto, Hecker monument, music stand, shaded walks, and lily pond, forms a favorite resort on the South Side."

Courtesy of NiNi Harris

The surrounding blocks are now part of a historic district named for Benton Park that began experiencing a remarkable rejuvenation in the 1990s. New residents in nearby houses treasure their views of the romantic park. The annual report on Benton Park from the spring of 1914 is as true today as it was then. It declared that the park's "beauty and attractiveness is one of the joys of the people living near this section on the south side, and has aroused a most appreciative neighborhood pride."

Founded	Size	Cost
1868	289 Acres	Gift of Henry Shaw

TOWER GROVE PARK

Courtesy of Mark Abeln

Courtesy of NiNi Harris

Tower Grove Park—filled with ornamental trees, giant shade trees, curving carriage drives, statuary, Victorian follies, and stone gates at every drive and walkway—seems like a mythical land. One of the finest examples of Victorian landscape in the nation, Tower Grove Park's nearly 300 acres also show traces of St. Louis's French heritage. Its long, narrow footprint reflects the east-west strips of the colonial-era common field that it was cut from.

Anglo-American businessman and philanthropist Henry Shaw donated the park to the people of St. Louis in 1868. In concert with St. Louis's premier mid-19th-century architect George I. Barnett, a fellow Anglo-American, Shaw guided its development during the next two decades. He believed that trees were "the grand ornaments of every rural scene, and much more conducive to the pleasure and enjoyment of the public than any artificial structures that can be erected by the hand of man." So he transformed the almost treeless prairie into a wooded landscape that today boasts more than 7,000 trees (representing 445 tree varieties) and 1,645 shrubs.

Between 1871 and 1873, Shaw and his team dotted the landscape with a dozen gazebos, or shelters. There are octagonal gazebos, gazebos topped with lacy ornamental ironwork, gazebos topped by cupolas, and gazebos with Gothic arches. One features an onion-domed roof, and another is fashioned after a Chinese pagoda.

Each of the park's 10 gateways is unique. Sculptures of griffins and sleeping lions top the stone piers of the east carriage gate. The castle-like west carriage gate has 40-foot-tall crenellated stone towers. This Gothic-style gate reflects the Victorian fascination with the chivalrous tales of knights. Shaw salvaged the smooth stone columns of the north gate from the Old Courthouse when it was being remodeled in 1870.

The most whimsical folly of the park is the mock ancient ruins that form the backdrop for the fountain pond. The ruins were built with architectural salvage from the burned Lindell Hotel in 1867. Statuary honoring musicians, writers, and scientists are focal points within the park.

The flower beds around statuary and gates are planted with ornamental grasses, canna lilies, castor beans, flowering tobacco, and other plantings popular during the Victorian era.

Courtesy of Mark Abeln

A series of amoeba-shaped lily ponds are filled with fragrant water lilies that bloom each September.

The park's trees, flower beds, and historic buildings were restored and are now maintained in Victorian style with a combination of city funds and the generosity of the supporters and Friends of Tower Grove Park.

In 1989, Tower Grove Park attained nationwide recognition when it was declared a National Historic Landmark.

In recent years, another feature of the park's historic landscape was restored—the eastern stream. It had been buried before 1913, leaving small stone pedestrian bridges crossing only dry creek beds. In 2022, the stream was daylighted and flanked with rain gardens featuring native plants. The restored stream—which snakes through the landscape—decreases flooding by capturing the heavy rain waters from 43 acres of the park. The stream is named Nee Kee Nee, meaning "revived water" in the language of the Osage people who once inhabited the land.

While the museum-like quality of the park now attracts visitors from around the nation, its appeal to generations of St. Louisans continues to be almost magical. During the early 20th century, the delightful Victorian features of the park provided the setting for Sunday afternoon strolls or evening bible study classes. A century later, they continue to provide the backdrop for St. Louisans' family and community life. Wedding photos are posed in front of the ruins. Parties are hosted in the 19th-century orangery (the Piper Palm House). A farmers market held in the park attracts thousands. The weekly Tower Grove Farmers Market, launched in 2006, has grown to a hundred vendors.

Henry Thiele, Francis Tunica, and Eugene Greenleaf formed a team of architects who assisted Henry Shaw and George I. Barnett in developing the park.

Images courtesy of Mark Abeln

Founded	Size	Cost
1876	1,293 Acres (originally 1,380)	$849,058

FOREST PARK

Courtesy of Steve Tiemann

Courtesy of Mark Abeln

Courtesy of Mark Groth

Fifty thousand people gathered on June 24, 1876, to dedicate Forest Park. Many thought paying $849,058 for a nearly 1,400-acre swath of land on the unpopulated outskirts of St. Louis was wasteful foolishness. Forest Park, however, would enrich life for generations of St. Louisans. It would become home to our cultural institutions and evolve into one of the nation's great urban jewels. After a massive $100 million park restoration that began in the mid-1990s, Forest Park reigns as the nation's stellar urban park.

St. Louisans began promoting the idea of an expansive park while Confederate armies still threatened the city. There were debates and legal actions, but park promoters would not be deterred.

They chose an immense tract of rolling terrain, its contours broken by hills and covered by virgin forest. Only a few neglected farms and abandoned huts of coal miners defaced the vast expanse of natural forest.

The landscape architect of Lafayette Park, Maximillian Kern, designed improvements for Forest Park. The result was a driving park with winding roads, rustic bridges, and lakes. Bandstands, pagodas, and picnic grounds interspersed the sylvan setting.

The park was chosen as part of the site of the Louisiana Purchase Exposition, and construction began in 1901. For the Fair, the park's western half was transformed into a veritable fairyland of white palaces surrounded by lagoons and artistic landscaping that extended west to Big Bend Boulevard. The magnificent spectacle attracted 20 million visitors.

Afterward, the famous landscape architect George Kessler guided the artful reconstruction of the park that included four great memorials from the Fair—the World's Fair Pavilion completed at a cost of $40,000 in 1909; the Fair's Fine Arts Palace designed by Cass Gilbert, which became the Saint Louis Art Museum; an equestrian statue of St. Louis known as the "Apotheosis of St. Louis" presented in 1906; and, in 1913, the Jefferson Memorial. The massive birdcage was preserved from the Fair. One by one, cultural institutions moved to or opened in the park.

Images courtesy of Mark Abeln

When Dwight F. Davis became park commissioner in 1911, he focused on athletics and recreational facilities. In Forest Park, he added 32 tennis courts in 1912. Spreading lawns were transformed into soccer and baseball fields. He guided construction of an additional golf course. While golf was known as a rich man's game, a Forest Park tournament attracted players from the most exclusive country clubs as well as from the professions, stock rooms, and machine shops. In 1918, the cost of maintaining the golf courses came to just over 6 cents per game.

Davis established a tradition of recreational use. By 1929, the park was home to 38 tennis courts, two public golf courses, 20 baseball diamonds, two soccer fields, two handball courts, a croquet course, a cricket lawn, and an archery range.

Massive tree planting restored the forest canopy to the former fairgrounds. By the spring of 1934, Forest Park's trees numbered 45,450, in varieties "too numerous to mention," according to city forester Ludwig Baumann.

Following the Second World War, the cultural institutions located in Forest Park thrived: the Saint Louis Art Museum

Courtesy of Mark Abeln

Courtesy of Mark Groth

located in the Fair's Fine Arts Palace; McDonnell Planetarium dedicated in 1963 and transferred to the Saint Louis Science Center in the 1980s; the Missouri Historical Society located in the Jefferson Memorial; the Muny Opera, which opened with *Aida* in 1917; and the Saint Louis Zoo, organized in 1911.

Forest Park, however, suffered slow decline. Suburban and sprawl development spread the population and taxpayers over a large metro area, but only the citizens within the limited St. Louis City boundaries supported the park and its institutions. In 1972, voters established the Zoo Museum District. As a result, city and county residents supported the Zoo, Art Museum, and later the Science Center and History Museum with their tax dollars.

The park itself, however, was supported only by city residents, a fraction of the population using it. During the 1950s, 250 city employees worked full-time in Forest Park. By the 1970s, only 25 part-time employees maintained the huge park.

In the mid-1980s, the city of St. Louis established Forest Park Forever, a nonprofit organization dedicated to restoring, maintaining, and sustaining Forest Park. The city and Forest Park Forever worked with thousands of citizens to develop a master plan for the park that was adopted in 1995. The plan adapted the park's facilities to new needs while restoring historical features and enhancing the natural environments.

Fountains and formal balustrades were added to the Grand Basin at the foot of Art Hill. Using the natural terrain, the water features—lakes, streams, waterfalls, and fountains—were expanded while water use was cut in half. Savannahs and prairies were restored, adding habitat for wildlife. The park's trees currently number about 47,000. More than 16,000 of the trees grow in mowed or manicured areas. More than 30,000 trees in natural areas provide lush canopies and a rich environment for a growing variety of birdlife.

Recreational features—including basketball courts, soccer fields, and trails—were added, expanded, or improved.

The result is that Forest Park sparkles, dazzling more than 15 million visitors each year.

Founded	Size	Cost
1876	179.7 Acres	$140,570

CARONDELET PARK

Courtesy of Mark Abeln

Courtesy of NiNi Harris

The waves and swells in the landscape shaded by century-old trees give Carondelet Park, at the city's southeast corner, its distinctive character. The park—destination of thousands of 21st-century bicyclers, walkers, and soccer players—was dedicated on July 4, 1876, as one of the trio of large parks developed in the 1870s.

To assemble the acreage, the city purchased land from speculators. Except for Alexander Lacy Lyle's elegant, white-frame antebellum home at the center of the park, the land was undeveloped.

A picnic pavilion was built, and private donations funded an artificial boat lake in the 1890s. The park's natural features, however, were its attractions. A *Souvenir of Carondelet*, published in the early 1890s, noted the park's "noble growth of oak, walnut, and hickory trees." The land itself was exotic, with sinkholes that had formed over the centuries as the underlying limestone slowly eroded. In 1900, the park's annual report described the grounds as "an ideal place for a park, with its high elevation, undulating surface, natural grottoes, springs, and sink holes."

Over the next four decades, the city gradually added features and architectural amenities to the park's natural attractions. The water surface area of the boat lake was doubled in 1909. Three years later, a series of eight sinkholes were hooked together to create the quarter-mile-long Horse Shoe Lagoon.

In 1913, the Arts and Crafts–style Grand Boulevard viaduct was constructed at the park's entrance. The city began building the handsome two-story boathouse overlooking the lake in 1918. The 1920s saw the construction of the Arts and Crafts–influenced, two-story, brick stables with extended eaves supported by wood brackets.

During the Great Depression, WPA workers further improved the park with their distinctive stonework. Their features included stone walls, stone steps leading to the lake, and a charming stone bridge over Horse Shoe Lagoon.

The park became a favorite setting for school picnics during the mid-20th century. For generations, Carondelet Park has hosted family reunions and has been the place where senior citizens teach their grandchildren to fish. The new millennium has seen expanded amenities in Carondelet Park, while neighborhood volunteers are securing its historic and natural attributes for the future. Thousands of citizens use the Carondelet Park Rec Complex, opened in 2009 near the old soccer and softball fields. The Friends of Carondelet Park, which numbers a hundred volunteers, worked with GORC (Gateway Off-Road Cyclists) to design and build the park's mile-long mountain bike trail that is surrounded by untamed nature. The volunteers sculpted the trail to switch back and forth as it passes between tree trunks or descends along gullies or around tree-circled sinkholes.

To protect the old-growth trees, volunteers with the Friends cut parasitic honeysuckle and other invasive vines off the trunks of towering trees. Working with Forest ReLeaf of Missouri, the Friends planted 500 new trees in 2024 alone, to ensure the lush, green canopy sheltering Carondelet Park remains for future generations of fishermen and picnickers.

Courtesy of Mark Abeln

Courtesy of Mark Abeln

Founded	Size	Cost
1876	127 Acres (originally 158)	$259,065

O'FALLON PARK

Courtesy of Mark Abeln

A placid lake, reflecting its sprawling Florentine-style boathouse, graces O'Fallon Park—one of a trio of parks established on the outskirts of St. Louis in 1876. This North Side park offered "a prominent position on the bluffs, and a commanding view of the extensive valley and waters of the Mississippi," according to L. U. Reavis's 1875 book *Saint Louis*. Since the construction of I-70 in 1954, the well-treed hills of the park can be recognized rising on the west side of the interstate.

The parkland was part of the estate of the late Colonel John O'Fallon. A veteran of the War of 1812, O'Fallon became an assistant Indian agent in St. Louis. He prospered as a sutler, or contractor supplying the frontier army. O'Fallon invested wisely in early railroads, the gas company, and in real estate. He built his own brick country home atop the hills that are now parkland and named it Athlone in honor of his father's hometown in Ireland. Excavation for the home uncovered bones, arrowheads, stone axes, and utensils, indicating it was an Indian mound.

The city purchased 158 acres from O'Fallon's children. The site is complemented by adjacent Bellefontaine and Calvary Cemeteries. The Rural Cemetery Movement, which introduced landscape design to cemeteries, inspired the development of both these institutions. Their monuments melted into the landscapes as the roads followed the natural contours of the land.

O'Fallon Park became a destination for carriage rides, as evidenced by the installation of fountains to water horses in 1893. The lake, constructed two years later, covers 6.5 acres. It featured a landscaped island. Later, a stone wall was built around the island to stop erosion, and it became one of the lake's decorative features.

Courtesy of Mark Groth

Glens, picturesque ravines, a turn-of-the-century observatory, tennis courts, and ball fields turned the park into a mecca for pleasure seekers. Permits document the early 20th-century popularity of the park—289 picnic permits and over 2,000 permits for the tennis courts were issued during the summer of 1911 alone. During 1912, O'Fallon Park was the scene of 45,525 tennis games.

The boathouse dates to 1913, and the two-story brick stable was constructed in 1925. The park's thick canopy included 4,463 trees, according to a 1934 survey.

While the donation of an abandoned adjacent cemetery added 8.5 acres to the park, the state took acreage for the construction of I-70.

Civic leaders see a new role for this historic park—as a catalyst for strengthening its surrounding historic neighborhood. As part of this vision, in 2011, 300 new trees were planted to ensure the park's forest canopy. New trails were constructed through the rolling acres of greenery. Two years later, the 76,000-square-foot O'Fallon Park Rec Complex opened. The great beauty of O'Fallon Park, however, remains its picturesque boathouse fronting its lake and ancient trees.

Founded	Size	Cost
1917	60 Acres	Gift of David R. Francis

FRANCIS PARK

Courtesy of Mark Abeln

Francis Park is the keystone of the St. Louis Hills neighborhood. It is also where nature, recreation, art, music, and neighbors meet. Created in the 20th century in a setting influenced by the Art Deco Movement, this remarkable park bears a strong resemblance to Victorian-era Lafayette Park. Like its Victorian counterpart, Francis Park is square and designed for walking, not driving. It is surrounded by broad boulevards lined with impressive architecture.

Real estate developer Cyrus Crane Willmore used the park as a selling point for his lots and houses in the St. Louis Hills neighborhood. He reserved lots facing the park's corners for churches, which accent the park's design.

The parkland was mostly in a natural state in 1930 when Park Commissioner Fred Pape predicted that Francis was "destined to be one of the beauty spots of St. Louis." Sixty thousand dollars were dedicated to developing the park, including massive grading and tree planting. By the spring of 1934, the city forester reported that the trees in Francis Park numbered 2,458. With manpower supplied by the Civil Works Administration (CWA) and the Works Projects Administration (WPA) relief programs, the park commissioner reported in the spring of 1937 that Francis Park was 85 percent complete. More than 90,000 square feet of sidewalks and athletic facilities, including handball, horseshoe, and tennis courts, were constructed. The relief workers constructed a 400-foot-long rectangular lily pond that was filled with water lilies and their rosy bursts of color.

The park itself features old groves of Austrian pines, Scotch pines, and Norway spruce. There are abundant sycamores and giant pin oaks, which are the landscape signature of the neighborhood. Allées of bald cypress line the central walks framing the lily pond. The northeast corner of the park features a landscape with characteristic WPA stonework. A curving stone bench was built into a sloping hillside, and small, rustic stone bridges cross the rivulet streaming through that corner of the park.

In 1884, civic leader David R. Francis purchased farmland, including the park site, which had originally been part of a Spanish land grant. Francis is best remembered for his dynamic leadership as president of the 1904 Louisiana Purchase Exposition. His resume, however, included mayor of the city of St. Louis, governor of the state of Missouri, and secretary of the interior in the cabinet of President Grover Cleveland. While Francis was serving as ambassador to Tsarist Russia, he officially donated the parkland to the city.

A statue of a dapper David R. Francis, wearing a top hat and carrying a cane, stands in the center of the park. Beginning in 2002, residents commissioned a series of sculptures for the park. These sparkling mosaic-covered works inspired by fairy tales ornament the lily pond area. Residents sponsored their first Art in the Park fair in 2005, which is fostering more original art for Francis Park.

A neighborhood highlight of the holiday season is the Christmas tree lighting ceremony in the park. The tennis courts are busy in warm weather, and in cool weather neighbors gather around the firepits at the park's beer garden. There are markets in the park and evenings when people gather with telescopes to watch the stars together. The most common activity at the delightful 60-acre square filled with trees and rolling lawns, however, has stayed the same for decades. From sunrise to well after sunset, there is a steady stream of people walking around the park—people pushing baby carriages, some power walking, some walking dogs, and some leisurely strolling as they relish the landscape.

With its constant hum of activity, this park is the ultimate community common ground.

Park	Founded	Size	Cost
Bellerive	1908	5.6 Acres	$110,422
Christy	1910	32 Acres	$95,504

KINGSHIGHWAY PARKS

At the beginning of the 20th century, a series of new parks and boulevards were created as part of the Kingshighway Boulevard system. The Kingshighway system looped the city, connecting existing and adding new parks. The system began at Bellerive Park with its spectacular river views. The loop concluded at Bellefontaine Cemetery, adjacent to O'Fallon Park with its commanding view of the Mississippi. Kingshighway and its extensions—Holly Hills and Bellerive Boulevards—hooked together Forest, Carondelet, and Tower Grove Parks. Three more new parks—Bellerive, Christy, and Penrose—were designed as links in this emerald necklace.

The Kingshighway Boulevard system made each park more accessible to the entire region. Sadly, in the 1960s the construction of I-55 severed the boulevard system from its dramatic starting place, Bellerive Park.

View of river through arches at Bellerive Park
Courtesy of Mark Abeln

BELLERIVE PARK

Bluff-top Bellerive Park offers spectacular vistas of the Mississippi River. The park's main entrance is over a broad stuccoed bridge constructed in 1917. Ten years after the bridge was built, the city constructed the Mission-style pavilion with its trio of arches framing views of the river.

Park	Founded	Size	Cost
Christy Greenway	2005	1 Mile	Donated
Penrose	1910	51 Acres	$165,127

CHRISTY PARK

Wedge-shaped Christy Park was purchased in 1910 as part of the arc of parkland connecting Holly Hills Boulevard with Kingshighway. Christy Park and Boulevard followed a narrow creek bed valley. It evolved as a ribbon of trees, lawns, and fields. The 1934 Civil Works Administration survey reported that Christy Park already boasted 1,390 trees. In 1999, 16 acres of the park were renamed Joseph R. Leisure Park. A dedicated public servant, Leisure began his career as a grasscutter and rose to serve as the city parks commissioner. At the turn of the millenium, children of South City's Bosnian community especially enjoyed the playground in this park.

THE CHRISTY GREENWAY

This linear park designed for walkers and bikers follows the creek bed valley that connects Christy Park to the River des Peres Parkway. Historic Sts. Peter and Paul Cemetery and Gatewood Gardens Cemetery line part of the greenway. With their white and gray stones and monuments, they create a sculpture garden as a backdrop. The Christy Greenway is the work of the Great Rivers Greenway.

Christy Road
Courtesy of Mark Abeln

Penrose velodrome
Courtesy of Mark Abeln

PENROSE PARK

When the city purchased the acreage at North Kingshighway and Bircher as a North City link in the Kingshighway system, the surrounding area was undeveloped. The parks' report of 1912 envisioned that Penrose "will ultimately become a neighborhood park and play field, when the surrounding properties are improved with homes." A century later, the surrounding area is a historic neighborhood.

Kingshighway Boulevard and railroad tracks divide this park into quadrants. The Mathews-Dickey Club calls a quadrant home. In 1961, the Saint Louis Cycling Club built the one-fifth-mile velodrome, known as the Penrose Park Bowl, in one of the quadrants. The banked bicycle course was the scene of the 1962 National Cycling Championships. After falling into disrepair, enthusiasts recently raised the money to repave the track.

Founded	Size	Cost
1947	105 Acres	70 Acres donated, $52,000 for remaining acreage

WILLMORE PARK

Courtesy of Mark Abeln

Courtesy of Mark Abeln

The normally peaceful landscape of Willmore Park occasionally transforms into a joyously noisy place when the barking from the patrons of the dog park is added to the cheers from the ball fields and combines with the raucous honking from flocks of geese. Though it is one of the city's newest major parks, Willmore Park has already made lots of good memories. Neighborhood residents can't help but smile when they talk about Camp Willy Worm or Camp Funny Face, summer camps held in Willmore Park during the 1980s that taught city kids how to sail in catamarans on the park's lakes.

This long, sweeping park borders the St. Louis Hills neighborhood and is the companion park to the River des Peres Parkway. Willmore follows the inside of the River des Peres's broad curve. The River des Peres Parkway follows the outer bank of the stone-sided river channel, and its line of trees provide a backdrop of green vistas for Willmore Park visitors.

Willmore Park originated with Cyrus Crane Willmore, the developer of the St. Louis Hills neighborhood, who donated 70 acres on the perimeter of the neighborhood for the park. The real estate developer stipulated that the city acquire and dedicate the balance of the 105 acres, making Willmore Park the sixth-largest park in the city. The transfer of the deed to the land required that the city start clearing, grading, and landscaping the area on or before June 1, 1947. Willmore also stipulated that the strip of land never be used for an airport.

Landscape architect Stuart M. Mertz in association with Layton, Layton, and Rodes designed the park, locating the roadways around the perimeter.

The popularity of Willmore Park's playground, fields, bicycle and running trail, and picnic shelters is due to the rolling landscape. Groves of mighty trees shade its large lawns. Shimmering lakes, one covering three acres and the other covering five, seem constantly rippling with the maneuvers of dozens of ducks and geese.

Courtesy of Mark Abeln

GATEWAY MALL PLAZA

Courtesy of NiNi Harris

A long, narrow strip of parks and public spaces, planned and developed over a century, form downtown's Gateway Mall. It stretches along Market Street from the grounds of the Gateway Arch to the soccer stadium at the western edge of downtown. At the eastern end, the National Park Service maintains the Luther Ely Smith Park that connects the Gateway Arch with the Old Courthouse.

Immediately west of the Courthouse is 1.9-acre Kiener Plaza. Designed as a setting for concerts and gatherings, Kiener Plaza doubles as a site to relish great architecture. It offers stunning views of the Greek Revival–style Old Courthouse, framed by the 630-foot-tall stainless steel Gateway Arch. The Plaza's landscape directs attention to architect Philip Johnson's glittering postmodern Spire Headquarters Building and toward Louis Sullivan's Wainwright Building.

The first incarnation of Kiener Plaza was dedicated in 1962, when surface parking lots were transformed into grassy parkland. It honored 1904 Olympic runner Harry Kiener.

Kiener Plaza was reincarnated in 2017 with a checkerboard of 75,000 square feet of granite, concrete, and marble pavers; a grassy concert area; fountains; a large playground; and the planting of more than 140 new trees. A feature from the original plaza, the statue by Lithuanian immigrant William Zorach named *The Olympic Runner*, is a nostalgic focal point in the redesigned Kiener Plaza.

Citygarden covers two blocks, or the three acres of the Mall from 8th to 10th Streets. Funded by the Gateway Foundation, this interactive sculpture garden features modern and contemporary sculptures. Their backdrops are provided by fountains and native Missouri trees, shrubs, grasses, ground covers, and wildflowers.

Courtesy of NiNi Harris

The fountains include a six-foot cascade over native limestone, a splash plaza with 102 vertical jets, and a tilted granite disk that moves water gently from the base of a massive sculpture.

Richard Serra's sculpture *Twain* dominates the next block of the Mall. Its 40-foot steel panels were installed in 1982.

The Gateway Mall extending west from 12th Street to Union Station, known collectively as Memorial Plaza, consists of parks, fountains, and memorials. Poelker Park, Memorial Plaza, Kaufmann Park, and Eternal Flame Park create this grouping. Memorial Plaza originated with a plan in 1904 for impressive civic buildings connected by a central plaza. The plaza links and offers vistas of St. Louis's grand City Hall, Public Library, and Union Station. The $87 million bond issue of 1923 included development of this park space and the building of Soldiers Memorial at its heart. During the 1930s, dramatic Art Deco–style civic buildings were constructed around the plaza. Memorials honor St. Louis's firefighters, policemen, and St. Louisans who served in the Korean War and in World War II.

Aloe Plaza, the block facing Union Station framed by 18th and 20th Streets, was cleared to serve as a stage for the stunning Milles Fountain. Officially named *The Meeting of the Waters*, the fountain depicts the confluence of the Missouri and Mississippi Rivers. The great Swedish sculptor Carl Milles created the fountain with 14 bronze figures in a rectangular pool of black and salmon marble measuring 200 feet by 35 feet. When it was unveiled in 1940, the provocative fountain was considered scandalous.

Courtesy of NiNi Harris

Courtesy of NiNi Harris

Founded	Size	Cost
1908	131 Acres	$700,00

FAIRGROUND PARK

Courtesy of Mark Abeln

Fairground Park swimming pool
Courtesy of NiNi Harris

The castle-like facade of the old bear pits still guards the southeast corner of Fairground Park. It recalls the park's heritage as the St. Louis Agricultural and Mechanical Fairgrounds. Beginning in 1856, the annual fair drew visitors from across the region. In 1860, 150,000 people crammed the fairgrounds to see the Prince of Wales, the future King Edward VII of England. Eventually, the fairgrounds included an art gallery, racetrack, mechanical hall, and zoological gardens.

Competing with new attractions, the fair's popularity gradually faded. In 1908, the city bought the then-vacant fairgrounds and transformed them into a public park.

On July 15, 1913, the Parks Department opened a swimming pool surrounded by a sand beach in Fairground Park. The pool covered five acres, making it the largest outdoor pool in the world. The operating costs were considered high, $95 a day, but justified. More than a half-million men, women, and children used the pool in the first two months.

A 1949 confrontation between neighborhood African American and White youth over the desegregation of the park's swimming pool was an important test of public access in St. Louis's history. The bond issue that passed in 1955 paid for a new swimming pool, hard-surface tennis courts, and lighted baseball diamonds.

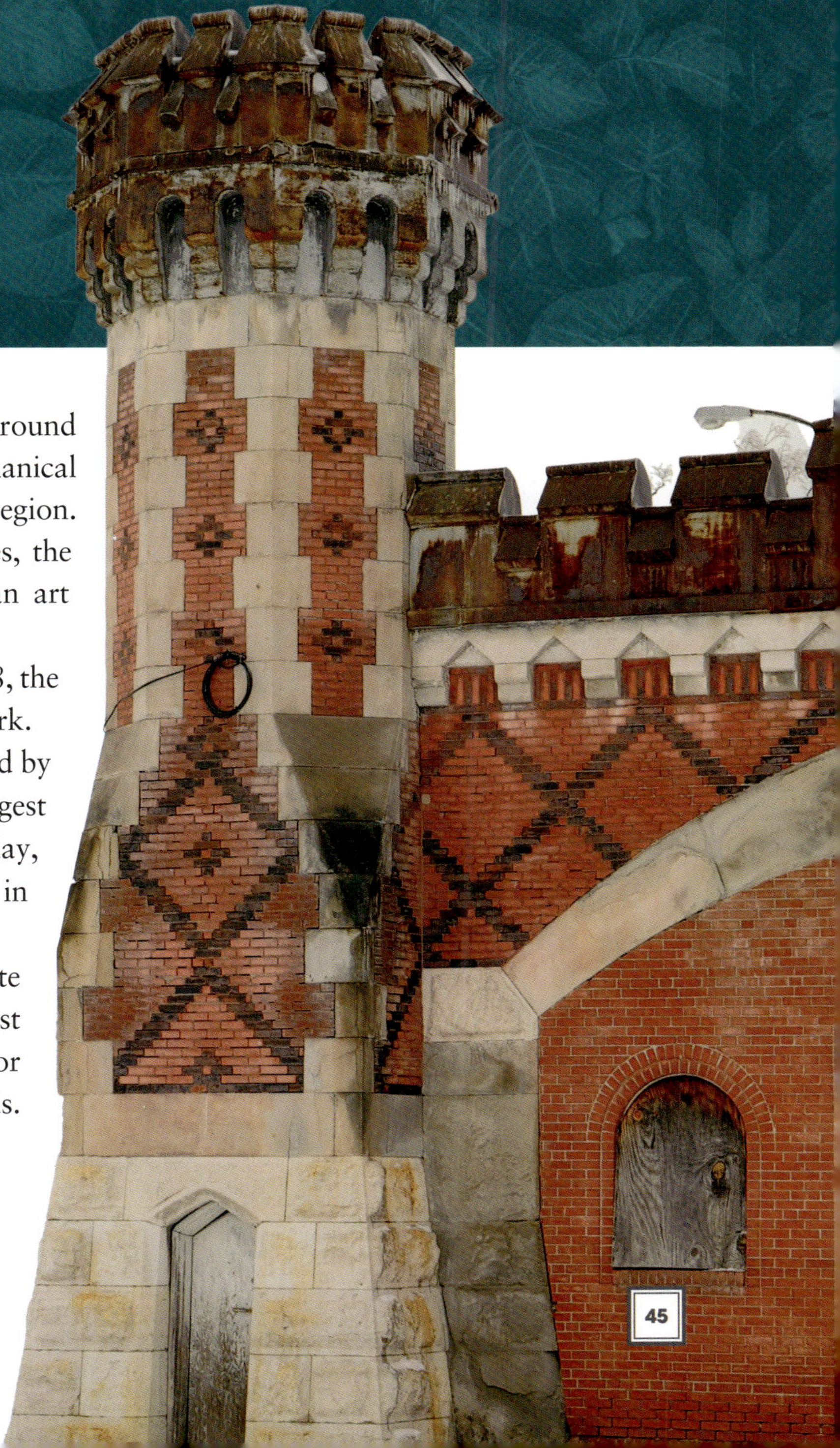

Courtesy of Mark Abeln

Founded	Size	Cost
1868	10.92 Acres	Gift of federal government

LYON PARK

Courtesy of Mark Abeln

Office workers from nearby industries and agencies treasure the quiet green acres of Lyon Park for walks and runs and as a lunchtime retreat. Facing South Broadway opposite castle-like Anheuser-Busch Brewery, this park slopes down to the complex of stone and brick buildings that still houses a division of the National Geospatial-Intelligence Agency. These acres, however, were not always the peaceful retreat between hubs of activity. For decades, the park acreage bustled and hummed.

Beginning in 1827, these acres were part of a US arsenal supplying the Armies of the West. Hundreds of laborers produced, repaired, and stored arms. They supplied Frémont's expeditions and American troops who battled in the War with Mexico.

The arsenal was a coveted prize at the beginning of the Civil War. Captain Nathaniel Lyon, an ardent abolitionist, commanded the arsenal, organized German volunteers for the Union Army, and protected the munitions. Activity at the arsenal increased as the war became more fierce and more costly. By 1865, a thousand men worked there.

The War Department transferred nearly 11 acres of the arsenal to the city for Lyon Park, memorializing the Union commander. The city planted lawns and shade trees and commissioned and installed the obelisk honoring General Nathaniel Lyon.

During August of 1913, area families brought mattresses and pillows to the park. Because it was in a crowded neighborhood with few yards, the park commission had designated Lyon as the South Side park to be used by sleepers on hot nights.

Courtesy of Mark Abeln

Founded	Size	Cost
1912	4.4 Acres	Donated

CLIFTON HEIGHTS PARK

Courtesy of Mark Abeln

Courtesy of Mark Groth

The origin of this saucer-shaped park set at the foot of rippled slopes mirrors that of 19th-century Methodist campgrounds. In 1885, a group of Methodists and their pastor, the Reverend Benjamin St. James Fry, bought 35 acres in what was then an isolated area of Southwest St. Louis. They commissioned St. Louis's premier designer of private places, Julius Pitzman, to survey and plat the area. He designed streets that curve irregularly to match the hilly terrain. In the style of the campgrounds, he left a large green, or commons, at the base of the valley. During the following decades, rambling frame houses were built on the slopes overlooking the idyllic commons.

The camp's commons was conveyed to the city in 1912 for a park. The Parks Department constructed a small lake. The annual report of 1913 described the inviting lake as "adding to the beauty of this little place." In the early 1920s, the city bought adjoining property, enlarging the park to its present size, 4.4 acres.

The department described the progress made in Clifton Heights Park in their annual report of 1928. "At last its beauty is completed. Nestling cozily in its luxurious growth and quaint surroundings it truly is one of the beauty spots in St. Louis."

The water system for the picturesque lake, however, created some unpleasantness in the neighborhood. This was corrected in 1944, when the Parks Department "overhauled water mains & valves, thereby eliminating objectionable noises in the private plumbing of the neighborhood homes."

HYDE PARK

Founded	Size	Cost
1854	12 Acres	$36,250

Courtesy of Mark Abeln

Courtesy of NiNi Harris

Only the gazebo with the onion-domed roof remains to recall the Victorian landscape that once filled this 12-acre square. Yet this small park is rich with history. When the city established Hyde Park, it marked a new dedication to creating a park system. All the earlier parkland had been donated or reserved from the old common fields. This was the first time the city was required to pay for parkland.

The park site had been part of the North Side real estate of Dr. Bernard Farrar, the first American physician to settle in St. Louis after the Louisiana Purchase. In 1850, his widow subdivided the property. The park and subdivision were apparently named for London's Hyde Park.

To pay for park improvements, the city rented the land—for a vegetable garden and then as a beer garden, with the old Farrar mansion serving as a hotel and inn.

During the Civil War, the park was the site of political and patriotic gatherings. On July 4, 1863, while great battles were being waged at Gettysburg and Vicksburg, thousands crowded into Hyde Park. The patriotic celebration devolved into a deadly riot between convalescing Union troops and Confederate sympathizers.

Landscaping of the park began in 1874. It was directed by Theodore Link, later known as the architect of Union Station. By the end of the Victorian era, an elegant fountain, an artificial lake, and a bandstand added to the park's allure.

The tornado of 1927 destroyed much of Hyde Park's Victorian character.

Courtesy of Mark Abeln

Park	Founded	Size	Cost
Pontiac	1908	1.9 Acres	$94,580
Soulard	1908	1.9 Acres	$174,580

SOULARD POCKET PARKS

Courtesy of Mark Abeln

Courtesy of Mark Abeln

The Soulard neighborhood boasts two delightful pocket parks—Soulard Park next to Soulard Market and Pontiac Park at 9th and Ann Streets. These parks, favorites with public gardeners and the neighborhood's many dog lovers, share a common origin. They were both proposed in the 1907 Civic Plan with the goal of providing playground areas in the then-overcrowded immigrant community.

A 1906 bond issue paid for the valuable land. The city cleared the commercial buildings, graded the blocks, and was operating playgrounds on them by 1911. The use of these parks was staggering. Between April 1919 and April 1920 alone attendance at playground activities numbered 128,024 children in Pontiac Park and another 74,117 children in Soulard Park. In 1938, the city used WPA workers and resources to build the stone terraces and retaining walls around the small parks.

As the neighborhood became revitalized in the late 20th century, the pocket parks took on new roles. Soulard Park hosts the annual Wiener Derby, or the Daschund race, held after the dog parade, kicking off the Mardi Gras celebration.

Beginning in 1990, volunteers with the Soulard Restoration Group gardened these parks and gave Pontiac Park a unique aesthetic. Volunteers filled beds and stone-edged terraces with flowering shrubs, ornamental grass, and evergreens. In Victorian fashion, neighborhood associations have framed these pocket parks with decorative iron fencing.

Parks	Founded	Size	Cost
Gravois Laclede Mount Pleasant	1854	8.2 Acres 3.17 Acres 3.17 Acres	Set aside from St. Louis Commons

DUTCHTOWN COMMONS PARKS

Gravois Park
Courtesy of Mark Abeln

Three small parks in the Dutchtown neighborhood of South St. Louis—Gravois, Laclede, and Mount Pleasant Parks—share a common history and role in their communities. These green and shaded squares serve their working-class, brick neighborhood as extended community backyards. Like backyards, two of the parks, Laclede and Mount Pleasant, face alleys.

Their origins date to 1812 when their neighborhoods were simply wilderness, miles beyond the fur-trading post of St. Louis. That year, the United States recognized public ownership of the French commons, land that had been jointly owned by early settlers of St. Louis. While the city of St. Louis was gradually selling the commons, civic leaders saved these three squares for public or park use.

Gravois Park, near Grand and Gravois, became home to a huge neighborhood Independence Day celebration beginning in 1910. The octagonal bandstand, in then new-style concrete construction with a Mission-tile roof, was built in 1924.

Little Laclede Park is near South Broadway and Gasconade Street. Neighbors enjoy its abundance of lawns and shade trees.

Mount Pleasant Park, near Michigan Avenue at Dakota Street, was originally called Dakota Park and became a popular playground for the children of the nearby Polish community. During the summer of 1917, attendance at this little park's playground surpassed 37,000.

Laclede Park
Courtesy of Mark Abeln

Founded	Size	Cost
1934	145 Acres	Donated

RIVER DES PERES PARK

Courtesy of Mark Abeln

Courtesy of Mark Abeln

This ribbon of green, which doubles as a boulevard, provides ball fields, playgrounds, and an enticing trail. Lush trees shade these features. A parkway following the outer bank of the River des Peres was first proposed more than a century ago and has evolved over three quarters of a century. Landscape architect George Kessler encouraged creating a parkway in a sweeping arc around the southwest border of the city in 1911. He wrote that the River des Peres Valley, from practically the Mississippi River to McCausland Avenue, offered "an opportunity . . . to establish a splendid parkway, that would supply a tie along the western border of the city that cannot be surpassed."

The city purchased the riverside acreage in 1934, and its initial development was completed during the Great Depression. Over 12,000 shrubs and more than 2,500 trees were planted along the linear park. Eight hundred American elm trees lined both sides of the driveway. In 1938, the Parks Department annual report stated, "A new parkway . . . immediately on the county border, has been completed and developed into a beautiful Parkway. This parkway ranges in width from 250 feet to 1,000 feet." The park and boulevard were extended south of Gravois, with an average width of 20 feet on each side of the driveway.

In 2005, the parkway's new tree-lined bike and hiking trails were completed. Along with stone entrances and gates featuring 44 stone columns, the 5.5-mile trail (including the Christy Greenway) features a 250-foot-long pedestrian bridge crossing the River des Peres. As part of the development of this trail, 1,718 new trees were planted.

The River des Peres Parkway is the city's fifth-largest park. With its new plantings, trails, and distinctive stone gateways, it has become one of the city's newest green meccas, attracting bicyclers from the entire region.

Courtesy of Mark Abeln

Founded	Size	Cost
1915	16 Acres	Donated

MARQUETTE PARK

Courtesy of Mark Abeln

Marquette Park, in the heart of the South Side's Dutchtown neighborhood, was the site of a makeshift hospital for Civil War soldiers and an orphanage. Later it was the scene of Olympic tryouts and a movie set.

A combination orphanage and reform school, the House of Refuge opened on the site in 1855. The Union Army confiscated some rooms in the institution for hospital space for convalescing Union soldiers wounded at the Siege of Vicksburg. After closing the orphanage, the Board of Children's Guardians gave the land to the St. Louis Parks Department in 1915.

The popularity of the pool at Fairground Park made clear the need for an open-air pool convenient to South Siders. Marquette swimming pool opened on July 8, 1916. Daily attendance that summer averaged 1,500. The pool served not only generations of South Siders, but it also hosted the water polo tryouts for the 1948 US Olympic team. In 1960, the pool was replaced with a new 165-foot-long L-shaped pool.

In 1921, crews of prisoners from the City Work House demolished the remaining orphanage buildings on the west half of the park to make way for tennis courts, trees, and athletic fields. Those fields became a film set for crews and actors re-creating soccer games for the 2005 release *The Game of Their Lives*. The movie chronicled the United States team—with six St. Louisans—that defeated the favored English team in the 1950 World Cup.

Courtesy of Mark Abeln

Park	Founded	Size	Cost
Lindenwood	1915	14 Acres	$81,000
Tilles	1957	29 Acres	$380,000

BABY BOOM AND OTHER CITY PARKS

Courtesy of Mark Abeln

The post–World War II baby boom spurred the postwar housing boom. Suddenly, on the southwest fringes of the city, contractors and carpenters were turning the lots and blocks, which had been left vacant during the Great Depression, into vibrant neighborhoods. The city created two new parks that serve as extended backyards in these baby boomer neighborhoods—Tilles and Lindenwood Parks.

Both parks host practices, games, and tournaments for recreation programs funded by propositions, numerous parishes and clubs, and the Judge Dowd Soccer League. Their athletic fields and courts are in almost continual use from mid-April through mid-December.

LINDENWOOD PARK

Lindenwood Park was part of a Spanish land grant made to Charles Gratiot in 1798. The parkland forms a shallow, three-sided, shady valley facing Jamieson Avenue. With baseball, softball, and soccer fields; tennis courts; a playground; and a roller hockey rink, Lindenwood Park offers recreation for all ages.

TILLES PARK

Tilles Park, facing the east side of Hampton Avenue, serves its 1950s vintage neighborhood with baseball, softball, and soccer fields; basketball, racquetball, tennis, and volleyball courts; a roller hockey rink; and playgrounds. The terrace near the Fyler Avenue border of the park features Frank Lloyd Wright–style stonework and rectangular flower beds that reflect the neighborhood's modern style.

The Campau subdivision, which was platted in 1952, forms the park's eastern border. The "Potter's Field," or city cemetery, occupied the ground opposite the park on Fyler since before the turn of the century. The bodies were moved around 1950 and the site developed as the 510-unit Hampton Gardens Apartments, which was completed in 1952.

The establishment of Tilles Park on Hampton is directly tied to the history of the park by the same name in St. Louis County. In 1932, Captain Tilles donated 58 acres at McKnight and Litzinger Roads for a city park in memory of his mother, Rosalie. The city was able to sell that park to the county system and use the money to buy the parkland on Hampton Avenue.

Park	Founded	Size	Cost
Berra	1945	4.8 Acres	$15,000
Carondelet Lions	1929	1.7 Acres	$15,458

BERRA PARK

The fire hyrdrants around Berra Park are painted red, white, and green to evoke the flag of Italy, announcing the Italian-American heritage of the surrounding neighborhood, The Hill. An Italian flag is even painted on a wall in the ball field's perimeter. A huge bust of Louis G. (Midge) Berra greets visitors at the main entrance to the park, a flat, square acreage filled with ball fields and a playground. The park was renamed for Berra, St. Louis's first Italian American to be elected to citywide office, in 1965. The park doubles as a festival grounds for neighborhood celebrations of the community's Italian roots.

Courtesy of Mark Abeln

CARONDELET LIONS PARK

Once the ball field for local Irish-American and German-American children, Carondelet Lions Park is now the front yard for the Temtor, an old Coca-Cola syrup plant that has been converted into loft-style apartments. The plant was built in 1919 for a fruit preserves company.

Irish St. Louisan and philanthropist Bryan Mullanphy purchased the parkland in 1843. He bequeathed the property to the Mullanphy Emigrant Relief Fund. Informally known as Mullanphy Park, it was renamed Carondelet Lions Park after the Lions Club of Carondelet worked with the city of St. Louis in grading, sodding, and installing the playground's first equipment in 1963.

Courtesy of Mark Groth

Park	Founded	Size	Cost
Chain of Rocks	1910	29.76 Acres	Transferred from Water Deparment
Cherokee	1924	8.9 Acres	$90,000

CHAIN OF ROCKS PARK

The Water Department purchased this forested river bluff in 1893 to protect the healthful setting adjacent to the waterworks. An amusement park, located on top of the bluff, spurred use of public picnic grounds from 1927 to 1978. The new St. Louis Riverfront Trail connecting with Downtown St. Louis and the renovated multi-use Chain of Rocks Bridge is again increasing the park's popularity with bikers and walkers.

CHEROKEE PARK

A private beer garden was operating on this acreage by the Civil War. Nearby Lemp Brewery then bought the garden and operated it as Lemp's Park, which hosted reunions of the Grand Army of the Republic. During Prohibition, the city used bond-issue money to buy the land and turn it into a public park. The State Highway Department cut off the corner of the park for the construction of I-55.

Courtesy of Mark Abeln

Park	Founded	Size	Cost
Columbus Square	1908	0.45 Acres (originally 2.16)	$236,641
Compton Hill	1867	35.8 Acres	$100,000

COLUMBUS SQUARE PARK

On July 17, 1914, Columbus Square was the site of the first "Municipal Movie" presented in a city park. The crowd of about 3,000 included "mothers and babies, fathers and small boys, Italians, Greeks, Poles, Jews, Irish, Germans and two-generation Americans." The half-acre square, established in 1908, is surrounded by a new downtown neighborhood.

COMPTON HILL RESERVOIR PARK

Following the Civil War, the city chose this acreage for a reservoir because it was the highest spot within the then–city limits. The Water Department maintained the surrounding acreage as a park, so the trees and plant life would filter the air around the open reservoir. By the turn of the century, groves of oaks shaded the east side, and floral displays highlighted the west side. The 175-foot water tower was built in 1898 at a cost of $48,000. On August 6, 1961, the Water Department turned over the maintenance of the surrounding park to the Parks Department. The construction of I-44 encroached on the northern border of the 35-acre park.

Courtesy of Mark Abeln

Courtesy of Mark Abeln

Park	Founded	Size	Cost
Fountain	1889	1.5 Acres	Gift of John Lay
Fox	1917	2.69 Acres	$85,000

FOUNTAIN PARK

A statue of Dr. Martin Luther King Jr., by sculptor Rudolph Torrini, overlooks this small, oval park surrounded by handsome brick homes. The statue was unveiled in the park in 1978. The developer of Aubert Place reserved this green oval at the center of the subdivision before the Civil War. In 1889, the oval became a city park.

Courtesy of Mark Abeln

FOX PARK

The big-league-style scoreboard reigns over the outfield of the Police Athletic League ball field in Fox Park. Cardinals Care, the charitable arm of the St. Louis Cardinals, and the late pitcher Darryl Kile funded the renovation of the ball field for use by the league and by neighborhood children. The park features a brick Italian-Romanesque-style shelter dating to the early 20th century.

Courtesy of Mark Groth

Park	Founded	Size	Cost
Jackson Place	1816	1.62 Acres	Gift
Lucas Gardens	1857	1.09 Acres	Gift of James H. and Marie E. Lucas

JACKSON PLACE PARK

Young evergreens ring little Jackson Park, the flat circle of ground facing I-70 that has a rich history. The founders of the town of North St. Louis, later annexed by the city of St. Louis, set aside the circle of land for public assembly and recreation. By the Gilded Age, an ornate, tiered, cast-iron fountain graced the center of the circle. Walks, benches, and substantial trees surrounded the fountain. As the neighborhood evolved into a crowded immigrant community, the circle became a busy playground. In 1902, 3,000 to 4,000 people passed through the circle daily, many on their way to streetcar stops.

Courtesy of Mark Groth

LUCAS GARDENS PARK

With its prominent location, block-sized Lucas Park has experienced extreme ups and downs but has a bright future facing the grand new entrance of the Main Branch of the St. Louis Public Library.

The park, a sunken garden, had been the site of the brick home built by Judge John B. C. Lucas in 1820. His descendants gave the land to the city as a "public Promenade." The park's delightful, ornamental drinking fountain was sculpted in 1915. During most of the 20th century the rectangular, sunken, formal gardens were a favorite spot to read a book just checked out from the adjacent library. The library piped light classical music into the park during lunch hours. With the renovation of nearby warehouses as lofts, new downtown residents spurred the creation of a dog park within Lucas Park. The park will continue to evolve since the renovated, Italian Renaissance–inspired library has a new entrance with an atrium and elegant fountain looking onto Lucas Park.

Park	Founded	Size	Cost
McDonald	1928	3 Acres	$12,650
Minnie Wood Square	1925	4.5 Acres	Gift of Minnie Wood Estate

Courtesy of Mark Abeln

MCDONALD PARK

McDonald Playground at Utah and Bent serves the Oak Hill neighborhood with its softball and soccer fields, and playground. This park was one of many small parks that the city established so that no child would have to walk more than a half-mile to a playground.

Courtesy of Mark Abeln

MINNIE WOOD MEMORIAL SQUARE

Young trees border Minnie Wood Memorial Square, with its busy athletic field. The tip of the wedge of parkland along South Broadway at Meramec Street was transferred from the Street Department to the Parks Department in 1910 and was called the Meramec Triangle. In 1925, the estate of Mrs. Minnie Wood purchased the adjacent 4.5 acres and donated them to the city for a playground. Minnie was a German immigrant who married an English immigrant. Together, they ran a boarding house for milk wagon drivers. She received a substantial settlement in their separation, which paid for the park. In 1927, the city built the Mission Revival–style shelter and a wading pool.

Park	Founded	Size	Cost
Terry Park	1945	4 Acres	$40,000
St. Louis Place	1859	14.13 Acres	Donated

ST. LOUIS PLACE PARK

A chain of four rectangular blocks that intersects St. Louis Avenue at 21st Street forms St. Louis Place Park. The original 10 acres were donated to the city in 1850. Park records state the land was a "Gift of John Miller, et al." The southernmost block, south of Benton Street, had been the site of an earthen, wood-lined water reservoir from about 1850 to 1870. During the late 20th century, polka music echoed through this park from the annual festival held at the adjacent Polish Falcons Hall.

Courtesy of Mark Abeln

Courtesy of Mark Abeln

TERRY PARK

This park site was the grounds of the home of James Buchanan Eads, the premier 19th-century Mississippi River engineer and builder of the Eads Bridge. The city named the park for a neighborhood resident, Dr. Robert Terry. Terry was a leader in the conservation movement. A new neighborhood, the Gate District, was built near Terry Park.

Park	Founded	Size	Cost
Sherman	1917	22 Acres	$196,560
Sister Marie Charles	1948	Nearly 1 Mile	

SHERMAN PARK

Sherman Park was the campus of Christian Brothers College, which burned in 1916. The site, facing Kingshighway, fit into the Kingshighway Plan of an emerald necklace of parks and boulevards circling the city. In 1917, the city purchased the property and converted the remaining school building into a community center. In 1959, a new recreation center was built facing Kingshighway.

Courtesy of Mark Groth

Courtesy of Mark Groth

SISTER MARIE CHARLES PARK

With overlooks resting on the riverbank, this park at the foot of Chouteau's Bluff and below Bellerive Park offers a rare opportunity to get close to the Mississippi River. This linear park provides walks between the limestone bluffs, the railroad tracks and the river. During high water, the barges rise to eye level with the walkways.

This section of riverbank was home to a Hooverville built during the Great Depression. Shanties raised on stilts stood on this site into the 1960s. Sister Marie Charles, director of Carondelet Community Betterment Federation Inc. and one of the Sisters of St. Joseph of Carondelet, lobbied for the creation of this riverside park.

Park	Founded	Size	Cost
South St. Louis Square Park	1882	1.66 Acres	Donated from the Hospital Division
Yeatman Square Park	1906	3.4 Acres	$40,000

SOUTH ST. LOUIS SQUARE PARK

South St. Louis Square was once a market square for its Carondelet neighborhood, which was an independent French village. The park has become a catchall for remnants and symbols of its community's varied history. The brick store building in the park's northeast corner was constructed as a public market just before St. Louis annexed Carondelet in 1870. The historic stone house in the park's southeast corner was built by Bavarian immigrant Anton Schmitt in 1859. (This house was moved to the park in 1992.) In 2011, local business leaders installed a replica of a 32-pounder, Civil War–era naval cannon to recall that James B. Eads constructed Union ironclads in Carondelet.

YEATMAN SQUARE PARK

Following World War II, thirty quonset huts were constructed on the site of Yeatman Playground to provide emergency housing for African American veterans returning to overcrowded St. Louis. The land was eventually returned to park use, but gradually, many of the surrounding houses were abandoned.

Courtesy of Mark Abeln

Park	Founded	Size	Cost
Sublette Park	1915	13.52 Acres	Donated from the Hospital Division
Tandy Park	1918	5.6 Acres	$102,380

SUBLETTE PARK

As children, big leaguers Joe Garagiola and Yogi Berra played baseball in Sublette Park. The triangular park had been the site of the Social Evil Hospital, later named the Female Hospital. The park occupies the highest point in the city.

Courtesy of Mark Abeln

TANDY PARK

The city purchased the acres at Pendleton and Cottage to create Tandy Park in the historic African American neighborhood, the Ville. The park was named for Civil War veteran Captain Charlton H. Tandy, a pioneer in African American education in Missouri.

During the 1920s, Tandy Field was home to four teams in the Colored Industrial League, including the Scullin Steel Mules and Pullman Shops Nine.

In an era of segregated playground programs, Tandy served African American children along with three other playgrounds: Carr, Columbus, and Gamble. Together, their attendance for the summer of 1934 was 223,274.

Courtesy of Mark Abeln

MORE CITY PARKS

Generations of civic leaders created scores of small parks so that squares of lawns and trees would be focal points of neighborhoods and all St. Louis children could walk easily to a playground. While not every such park has as distinctive a story as the featured parks, each one has provided health and happiness for St. Louis children over the decades. Some of the small parks that once served crowded neighborhoods are now underused, some are surrounded by vacant lots and empty buildings. However, as these parks were once lush centerpieces of community life, they can now spur neighborhood renaissances.

Aboussie Park
Courtesy of Mark Abeln

The city park system, in addition to the featured parks, includes:

Aboussie Park	0.4 acres
Alaska Park	4.7 acres
Amberg Park	2.8 acres
Amherst Park	4.4 acres
Barrett Brothers Park	13 acres
Beckett Playground	3.3 acres
Buder Playground	2.3 acres
Busche Park	6 acres
Carnegie Park	2 acres
Chambers Park	6 acres
Chouteau Park	1.2 acres
DeSoto Park	17.3 acres
Dickman Park	5.21 acres
Eads Square Park	4.2 acres
Eugene "Tink" Bradley Park	3.2 acres
Fanetti Plaza	1.7 acres
Father Filipiak Park	4.3 acres
Fourteenth Street Mall	1.27 acres
Francis R. Slay Park	9 acres
Frank Williamson Sr. Park (Parkland Park)	2.4 acres
Franz Park	4.7 acres
Fremont Park	2.3 acres
Greg Freeman Park	0.9 acres
Gregory J. Carter Park (formerly Dwight Davis Park)	9.6 acres
Gwen Giles Park	5.4 acres
Hamilton Heights Park	1.3 acres
Hickey Park	16 acres
Interco Plaza	0.71 acres
Ivory Perry Park	11 acres
Jet Banks Park	3.4 acres
Kingsbury Square Park	0.6 acres
Loretta Hall Park	2.3 acres
Marie Fowler Park	0.7 acres
Mestres Park	3 acres
Minnesota and Hill Park	0.5 acres
Murphy Park	10 acres
Norman Seay Park	3 acres
North Riverfront Park	250 acres *(when combined with Chain of Rocks)*
Phillip Lucier Park	3 acres
Ray Leisure Park	7.3 acres
River des Peres Extension	11 acres
Rumbold Park	3 acres
Russell Park	1.1 acres
Ruth Porter Mall	8 acres
Samuel Kennedy Park	1 acre
St. Marcus Commemorative Park	26 acres
Strodtman Park	1.7 acres
Taylor Park	0.3 acres
Tiffany Park	1.1 acres
Turner Playground	1.4 acres
Unity Park	2 acres
Vivian Astra Park	1.1 acres
W. C. Handy Park	12 acres
Walnut Park	2.3 acres
Washington Square Park	13.5 acres
Windsor Park	3.3 acres

In addition, the following parks—Adams Park, Blasé Park, Kiel Triangle Park, Leon Strauss Park, and Robert J. Baer Plaza—are operated by other civic and municipal entities.

COUNTY PARKS

Esley Hamilton

A steam locomotive along Creve Coeur Lake

A. P. Greensfelder (left) poses with Herman Barken in 1953. *Courtesy of St. Louis County Parks*

While the city of St. Louis created an outstanding park system in the 19th century, little thought was given to parks in St. Louis County until after the World's Fair, and then the impetus came primarily from progressive city interests. The Civic League proposed a city-county "public reservation district" in 1907. They hired landscape architect George Kessler to design a comprehensive plan of parks and parkways that would link scenic areas throughout the region. Kessler had successfully created such an integrated network in Kansas City. His Outer Park plan here highlighted the bluffs above Columbia Bottoms, Spanish Lake, Charbonier Bluff west of Florissant, Creve Coeur Lake, the Meramec Highlands of western Kirkwood and the bottomland below them now in Fenton, and the Jefferson Barracks US military reservation. Voters rejected the plan in 1910, and the Missouri Supreme Court ruled against the proposed regional district in 1913.

Florissant's Spanish Land Grant Park goes back to the founding of the community in 1786, when it was intended to be a marketplace and a site for the parish church. Bridgeton, another Spanish settlement, incorporated in 1843, followed by Florissant, Kirkwood, and Fenton, but they were surrounded by countryside and not in need of parks. University City, founded in 1906, was by contrast an extension of the fast-growing central city, and it seems to have been the first municipality to establish its own park system, beginning in 1920 with Lewis Park, the former backyard of the city's founder, E. G. Lewis. The Park Board worked with the School Board to purchase adjacent parcels, as at Flynn Park (1923) with Flynn Park School and Millar Park (1929) with Nathaniel Hawthorne School. Gradually, other cities set aside their own parks. Clayton opened Shaw Park in 1937, and Webster Groves voted the funds for Blackburn Park in 1945.

The city of St. Louis made an effort in the 1930s to establish a regional park system on lands it owned in the county, using Works Progress Administration and Public Works Administration funds from New Deal programs. C. A. ("Cap") Tilles, who had made his fortune through racetracks and off-track gambling, presented Tilles Park at McKnight and Litzsinger Roads to the city of St. Louis in 1932. It remained a city park until 1957. Fort Belle Fontaine and the Buder property across from Valley Park were also intended to be city parks. The state of Missouri entered the park scene in 1934 when Jacob and Henry Babler gave over 2,100 acres in memory of their brother. It was developed through another New Deal program, the Civilian Conservation Corps.

The first park to be presented to the county government was Creve Coeur Lake Park, dedicated in 1945 as a war memorial. Since the county had no parks department, Creve Coeur was managed by a board of trustees, for many years under the guidance of A. P. Greensfelder, a University City businessman who became a leading advocate of conservation and rational city and regional planning. When the Tyson Valley ammunition "dump" or storage facility was declared surplus by the federal government in 1947, the county was able to acquire a tract twice the size of Forest Park, but the Korean War a few years later required its return to the Department of Defense.

A new county charter replaced the old three-judge system in 1950 with a county superintendent (now called county executive) and county council. Article IV of the charter created a department of parks and recreation under a commissioner (later director). That same year, the county was able to acquire Sylvan Springs Park and the first part of Jefferson Barracks Park as surplus federal lands. West Tyson Park was reclaimed from the Tyson Valley site in 1955, and Lone Elk Park at the east end of that tract rejoined the park system in 1964 after a long struggle. The Parks and Recreation Advisory Board was set up in 1951.

County Supervisor Luman Matthews created the St. Louis County Historic Buildings Commission in 1957 by executive order, confirmed by ordinance in 1982. The federal gift of the former ordnance section of Jefferson Barracks required the county to set up a museum telling the military history of the base, and Matthews asked the commission to help with that. The Powder Magazine Museum opened in 1960. The first chairman of the commission was Charles van Ravenswaay, then the director of the Missouri Historical Society. As editor of the *WPA Guide to Missouri* and a noted expert on Missouri history, van Ravenswaay saw the commission's potential and emphasized its role in identifying and preserving the county's historic resources. The Historic Preservation Commission (known to the staff as the HBC) thus became the earliest local government preservation body in the state.

Historic Buildings Commission, 1966
Courtesy of St. Louis County Parks

Since its beginning, the park system has benefitted from the generosity of individuals who have donated both land and funds for facilities. Their stories are among the most interesting aspects of park history. Buder Park, for example, reflects the newspaper history of the region, as the Buder family at one time owned both the *St. Louis Times* and the German-language *Westliche Post*. The park came to the county in 1954 through provisions in the will of Gustavus A. Buder Sr., who had first given the land in 1917 to the city of St. Louis.

John Allen Love founded Prudential Savings and Loan of St. Louis. His wife, Mary Potter Love, was perhaps better known than he, as the first local woman to head her own real estate company. They gave Love Park in 1959, naming the picnic shelters after two of their daughters: Mary, who married Frederick Lehmann III; and Cynthia, called "Muffin," who married Ben Roth. Another park using a family nickname is Suson, which was acquired in 1962 from Sidney Salomon Jr., the first owner of the St. Louis Blues hockey team. The name comes from his two children Susan and Sidney III, called "Sonny."

While on the subject of names, it should be noted that two park names are the result of misprints. Forrest Staley Park is named for Forest H. Staley (1885–1941), who supported the Boy Scout troop that uses this property. The court order transferring the property to the county in 1980 added the extra "r." Bella Fontaine Park results from a 1960 query from the parks director to the mayor of Bellefontaine Neighbors. He suggested that the park name be written as two words, as it was in the 19th century. His secretary, however, typed "Bella," the Italian word for "beautiful," instead of the French "Belle."

The Bissell House, near Bella Fontaine Park, was a gift beginning in 1960 from Janet Bissell Dimond, the great-granddaughter of General Daniel Bissell. (The home of the general's nephew Lewis Bissell in the Hyde Park neighborhood had been saved in 1958.) Restoration was led by HBC member Carolyn McDonnell (Mrs. William S. McDonnell), who at the same time was leading the restoration of the Thomas Sappington House, owned by the city of Crestwood but also supported by the HBC.

Another member of the HBC, Leicester Busch Faust and his wife, Mary, gave 100 acres for Faust Park in 1968, including Thornhill, the home of Missouri's second governor, Frederick Bates. Mary's bequest doubled the park in 1996 and included her own home and other noteworthy buildings. Leicester Faust was a grandson of Adolphus Busch of Anheuser-Busch and also of Tony Faust, the most famous restaurateur in St. Louis at the turn of the 20th century. Norman Champ of the Champ Spring Company, along with his brother Joseph, gave the 49-acre Champ Park in 1971, then joined the HBC two decades later.

Howard C. Ohlendorf's company made supplies for orthodontists. He and his wife, Irma, made many gifts to the park system, including part of Ohlendorf Park and the 46-acre Ohlendorf Park West on Hanna Road. They donated fountains for the lakes at Tilles and Queeny Parks. Most importantly, they rescued the St. Louis Carousel from the old Forest Park Highlands Amusement Park in 1965 for Sylvan Springs Park, then 15 years later contributed generously to its restoration at Faust Park.

Real estate broker Edwin F. Bright gave his 19th-century Brightfield Farm complex south of Manchester in 1974. The park site remains undeveloped, but the barn and smokehouse are now part of the village at Faust Park. Bright became a local celebrity because of his mule Beulah, who was named World's Champion Riding Mule at a national show in 1971. Beulah and Bright were often featured in parades and represented Missouri in national bicentennial events in 1976. Bright donated the equestrian shelter at Greensfelder Park, which he was proud to say was the only shelter in Missouri and probably in the nation named for a mule. He died in 1979, but Beulah survived in the care of County Parks until her death in 1998. She is also remembered at Greensfelder by a trail and a campsite.

Charles R. Skow, a mayor of Brentwood, was elected to the County Council in 1950 and became the first official park commissioner in 1957. A shelter at Tilles Park was named in his memory after he died unexpectedly in 1962 at the age of 49. Skow was succeeded by Wayne C. Kennedy, the department's recreation supervisor who had won a national award from the National Recreation Association the previous year. Kennedy had been a teacher and administrator in the Mehlville (R-9) School District before becoming involved in recreation through leading a grassroots effort to construct the R-9 Community Center. In nearly 30 years as director of parks and recreation, Kennedy brought the system to essentially its present size and configuration.

He paid for this expansion from about 1,000 to more than 12,000 acres by continuing the bond issues that had been initiated by Greensfelder and Skow and by obtaining a wide variety of public and private grants. Bond issues passed in 1955 and 1959 permitted the development of several neighborhood sites. The bond issue of 1969 provided $25 million for the purchase of Queeny Park, the development of north, south, and west recreation complexes, and much more. Another bond issue in 1977 permitted the acquisition of McDonnell and St. Vincent Park, along with other sites, while the 1986 bond issue provided funds for the Fountain Lake sports complex at Bella Fontaine, the community center at St. Vincent, a memorial to military veterans at Jefferson Barracks, and other projects.

Funds from bond issues were often used to match federal grants, especially from the Interior Department's Land and Water Conservation Fund, which is generated by revenues from leases for offshore oil and gas drilling. Parklands acquired or developed with these funds cannot be diverted to other uses unless replaced in kind. Bond issue funds were also matched by private foundations. A. P. Greensfelder's generosity continued after his death in 1955 through foundations he organized. One of them, St. Louis Regional Planning and Construction, gave Greensfelder Park in 1963, while the Albert P. Greensfelder Foundation funded the Greensfelder Recreation Complex in Queeny Park.

Groups of citizens coming together to support one particular park have become increasingly important. The Transport Museum Association (TMA) has aided the Museum of Transportation since 1948. Laumeier Sculpture Park has its own board and staff. Several groups operate under the umbrella of the Historic Sites Foundation of St. Louis County, a charitable organization whose only members are its board of three people. One such, the Friends of the Carousel, has expanded its focus to become the Faust Cultural Heritage Foundation. The Friends of Jefferson Barracks is another. The Open Space Council was organized in 1965 as an independent organization with many conservation interests, but it has often assisted the county, most critically in 1968 when they raised the matching funds to the rescue of the Nims Estate, Bee Tree Farm, now Bee Tree Park. The house designed by Frank Lloyd Wright for Ruth and Russell Kraus was saved in 2001 after a six-year campaign by citizens, and they now administer the facility as the Frank Lloyd Wright House in Ebsworth Park.

Left: Ed Bright and Beulah. Center: Dedication of Buder Park monument. Right: Leicester Busch Faust, his daughter Ann, and granddaughters
Courtesy of St. Louis County Parks

Mr. Kennedy, as he was called by staff, gained a reputation for his ability to awaken the generosity of donors. In response to his efforts, for example, Matilda Laumeier (called "Pink" by the family) bequeathed her estate in Sunset Hills in memory of her husband, Henry. Ethel Queeny, who with her husband, Edgar, had sold their large estate near Town and Country to developers, later changed her mind and contributed over a million dollars to its development as a park. Cap Tilles had given Jeanette L. Windegger a life tenancy in his house at Tilles Park, and she remained there from 1932 until the late 1970s, when she decided to move out so that the beautiful Windegger Shelter could be built on the site. A few of Kennedy's efforts did not end as hoped, however. Delbert Wenzlick died of a heart attack in 1979 while discussing the possible donation of his White Haven estate. Lee Hunter of Hunter Engineering talked about bequeathing his Hunter Farm estate on Ladue Road but failed to make any provisions before his death in 1986.

Kennedy also knew how to work with companies that were extracting sand and gravel from along the Meramec River. Winter Brothers Material Company donated George Winter

Park near Fenton in 1971 and Robert Winter, an undeveloped site on the opposite side of the river, in 1983. Simpson Sand and Gravel Company made a partial donation of the Simpson Park site in 1976. The excavations these companies made have been transformed into picturesque water features.

By the late 1960s, the county had several parks that might be considered cultural attractions, including Bissell House, the museum at Jefferson Barracks, and the children's farm at Suson. Laumeier Park, originally intended to be a nature study area, became a sculpture park in 1976, one of the first in the nation. The Museum of Transportation became a county park in 1979. Founded in 1944, it had assembled nationally significant collections that exceeded its ability to maintain. A more controversial museum appeared in 1985 when the Museum of the Dog moved from New York City to the historic Jarville House in Queeny Park. Since 1995, it has been affiliated with the American Kennel Club. The restored St. Louis Carousel opened in a climate-controlled building at Faust Park in 1987, emphasizing its status as a valuable work of American art.

Golden Eagle River Museum, a volunteer organization dedicated to preserving riverboat lore, occupied the Nims Mansion at Bee Tree Park until 2004 when it distributed its collections to other institutions. The National Civilian Conservation Corps Alumni Association restored a building at Jefferson Barracks originally built in 1898 as quarters for two officers but then moved to Virginia in 2008. The park system's newest museum is the Missouri Civil War Museum, whose organization worked for 10 years to restore the old Post Exchange and Gymnasium Building at Jefferson Barracks.

The range of activities in the parks reflects Mr. Kennedy's philosophy. He argued that in a culture as diverse as ours nothing was of interest to everyone but that everyone was interested in something. The broader the range of opportunities the parks could provide, the richer the experience for everyone. In practice this meant that park management had to remain alert to changing interests. The mini-bike park at Antire Park and the go-kart track at Widman Park have gone away, while model planes are still being flown at Buder Park

Courtesy of St. Louis County Parks

Courtesy of St. Louis County Parks

Courtesy of St. Louis County Parks

Top: Jeannette L. Windegger. Center: John Allen Love and Wayne Kennedy. Bottom: Henry and Matilda Laumeier.

Robert J. Hall
Courtesy of St. Louis County Parks

and Frisbee golf is gaining in popularity at Jefferson Barracks. Special events have also varied over the years, and some that once attracted thousands are now history. The Meramec River Raft Race was not really a race but a slow progression down the Meramec River from Unger to Winter Park, with prizes given for the most interestingly decorated vessels. The Haunted Forest was a pre-Halloween event that led hayrides past a series of scary features at Tilles Park. Mud Mania was an obstacle course for children that was guaranteed to result in the dirtiest possible participant.

Robert J. Hall, who became director of parks in 1995, was particularly attuned to changing park interests after 22 years managing the recreation division of the department. He was particularly aware of the intertwined interests in walking, hiking, and biking and in protecting scenic riverways. The Meramec River Recreation Association, active since 1972, was already a model of how intergovernmental cooperation can safeguard such resources, and the county's contribution included the Walston Chubb Trail on the south bank of the river and the Al Foster Trail on the north bank. The Danforth Foundation's "St. Louis 2004" initiative presented an opportunity to create a regional park and recreation district for these purposes. Hall resigned from the county in 1999 to lead this effort, which culminated in November 2000 with the passage of Proposition C. It created the Great Rivers Greenway District, a new unit of government in St. Charles County and St. Louis City and County with its own dedicated sales tax channeling funds to park, trail, and riverway projects at the regional, county, and city levels.

While parks consistently receive the greatest popular support of any county functions, relations between the department and the public have not always been happy. One particular source of antagonism has been the conflict over how or whether to develop Queeny Park. After battles in the 1960s and 1970s, this culminated in 1986 with a referendum to limit development in five so-called Heritage Parks: Cliff Cave, Greensfelder, Pelican Island, Queeny, and Saint Stanislaus. Partly as a result of that, the county gave Pelican Island to the Missouri Department of Conservation and turned over Saint Stanislaus on a long-term lease.

Other park properties have been transferred to other jurisdictions over the years. As the county's emphasis has shifted from small neighborhood playgrounds to multiuse regional parks,

Greensfelder Park
Courtesy of Steve Tiemann

Jarville House at Queeny Park
Courtesy of St. Louis County Parks

and as more cities have created their own park systems, 15 parks have been turned over to local jurisdictions. White Haven, saved from demolition in 1986 by a joint effort of the county and the Missouri Department of Natural Resources, became Ulysses S. Grant National Historic Site, a unit of the National Park Service, in 1990. Only a few developed parks have been lost: Grandview in Sunset Hills was taken in 1962 by I-270. Airport expansion eliminated Fairmount playground. The Page Avenue Extension took about about 40 acres of Creve Coeur Lake Park, but federal highway and open-space regulations required its replacement with more than 1,000 acres of new parkland, making Creve Coeur the largest park in the system.

After half a century of almost uninterrupted growth, the county park system found itself increasingly challenged as it entered the 21st century. Voters narrowly rejected a 2004 proposal to establish a dedicated sales for county parks. The next year cuts to the park budget nearly eliminated history programs in the parks and would have closed the museums at Jefferson Barracks

Aerial photograph of Jefferson Barracks
Courtesy of the Library of Congress

had not the Friends of JB agreed to staff them with volunteers. Since then park budgets have been in survival mode, buoyed only by funds from the regional park tax that permit playground and trail improvements to continue. The budget proposed for 2012 initially called for the permanent closure of 23 parks. As passed, the budget keeps these parks open but cuts nearly 14 percent of the department's funding. The principle that parkland should be inviolable is being challenged, as a 911 telephone facility is built in Ohlendorf West and half of Sylvan Springs Park is sold to Jefferson Barracks National Cemetery. The County Department of Highways plans to run the Northwest Parkway across Saint Stanislaus Park and Charbonier Bluff (still not secure after a century), while the South County Connector will go through the River des Peres Parkway. The need for the public to defend the county's cherished legacy of parks has never been greater.

Founded

1945

Size

2,114 Acres

CREVE COEUR LAKE PARK

Courtesy of Steve Tiemann

Courtesy of Steve Tiemann

Creve Coeur Lake Park is St. Louis County's first, largest, and busiest park, with over a million visitors annually. The lake was once a bend in the Missouri River. A second lake silted up early in the last century, and siltation reduced the big lake to an average depth of only 18 inches before it was rescued by a major dredging operation from 1974 to 1981.

French settlers were calling the lake Creve Coeur before 1800. The phrase means "broken heart" and describes a great grief, sorrow, or affliction. What it refers to here is unknown. It could refer to several places or families in France, a fort in Illinois, or even a breed of chicken but certainly not the spurious 19th-century tale of an Indian maiden.

The lake became a resort area in the 19th century. Railroad lines were extended by the Missouri Pacific in 1881 and the rival Katy in 1886. Hotels, dance pavilions, and boat houses were built, and in 1889 Jacob Studt offered grounds and a subsidy for the annual county fair. It was held here for about 30 years. The outline of the racetrack used then can still be discerned. A streetcar line opened from the Delmar Loop in 1899, and the brick electric station remains in the upper park.

The Creve Coeur Park Soccer Complex opened in this part of the park in 2018, with 14 soccer fields, including one championship field with seating for up to 500 spectators, 12 additional synthetic turf soccer fields, and one natural grass super pitch.

Courtesy of Steve Tiemann

That was also the site of a large amusement park known as Electric Park, which featured a 255-foot observation tower moved from the 1904 World's Fair. The lake declined in the 1920s as gangsters began to frequent the clubs along the lakefront and a poor residential subdivision was developed.

A revival began in 1945, when a group of citizens led by A. P. Greensfelder donated 400 acres to the county as a war memorial. The county then lacked a parks department, so a special administrative board was set up. The 1969 bond issue permitted the county to purchase all the land surrounding the lake, including the old subdivision with about 150 cottages.

The extension of Page Avenue across the south end of the lake in the 1990s controversially took 25.8 acres of parkland. In return, the park gained 1,005.8 acres west of the lake as well as many improvements, including trails, soccer fields, and a restaurant. Mallard Lake has been created to help control siltation, and 500 acres on the site of the Upper Lake are being returned to wetland.

Courtesy of Steve Tiemann

Courtesy of Steve Tiemann

Courtesy of Steve Tiemann

Courtesy of Steve Tiemann

Founded
1967

Size
197.39 Acres

FAUST PARK

Courtesy of Mark Groth

Butterfly House
Courtesy of Steve Tiemann

On its relatively small 200 acres, Faust Park concentrates some of the most fascinating historical sites and busiest recreational attractions in the metropolitan area. The park began as a gift from Leicester Busch Faust and his wife, Mary, in 1968 and was doubled in size by a bequest from Mary Faust in 1996.

The land was part of the Thornhill estate acquired by Frederick Bates (1777–1825) in 1808 and 1809. Bates had come from Virginia at the request of Thomas Jefferson to be secretary for the Upper Louisiana Territory. He built his two-story timber-frame house about 1818 for his mother and siblings, marrying 17-year-old Nancy Opie Ball the next year. Bates succeeded Missouri's first governor Alexander McNair in 1824, but he died the following year at the age of 48. He is buried in the family plot behind the house.

The Thornhill complex, including the main house, the two barns, granary, and other outbuildings, was listed in the National Register of Historic Places in 1974. Architect Richard Bliss restored the house, and it opened for tours in 1990. The peach orchard and log distillery building reflect the farm's original cash crop, peach brandy.

The St. Louis Carousel opened at Faust Park in 1987. It was created by the Gustav Dentzel Company of Philadelphia about 1920 and erected at Forest Park Highlands Amusement Park in 1929 with 64 hand-carved animals and two chariots. Howard Ohlendorf donated the carousel to St. Louis County in 1965. First used outdoors at Sylvan Springs Park, it reopened in its own building on May 9, 1987, following a privately funded restoration. That event was celebrated by the first St. Louis performance of Circus Flora, which has since become a St. Louis fixture.

The village of historic buildings in the park began in 1986 and has now grown to four residences, the Fenton Mercantile, the Alt School, the African School #4 from Chesterfield, and the Spanish Lake Blacksmith Shop, along with two barns and other outbuildings. The Miles Seed Carriage House from Jennings is now the park's visitor center. The City of Creve Coeur donated two log houses to the park in 2024.

Courtesy of Steve Tiemann

The Fausts' own residence was built in 1919 to Pueblo Revival designs by St. Louis architect Tom P. Barnett. He also designed the secondary residence and a dovecote. Maritz, Young & Dusard enlarged the house in 1935–36 and added the chateau-like garage. The unique 1925 barn was the first building in the region to use the lamella truss structural system.

The Sophia M. Sachs Butterfly House and Education Center, designed by Christner Inc., opened in 1998 and became a division of the Missouri Botanical Garden in 2001. The site includes an outdoor butterfly garden and two large sculptures by St. Louisan Robert Cassilly.

The county's largest playground opened at Faust in 2006. ADA-accessible, it has continued to attract record numbers of users.

Founded

1985

Size

293.17 Acres

FORT BELLE FONTAINE

Courtesy of Steve Tiemann

Courtesy of Steve Tiemann

Connecticut native Daniel Bissell (1768–1833) came to St. Louis in 1808 when he was appointed commanding officer of Fort Belle Fontaine by Thomas Jefferson. By the time he departed for active duty in the War of 1812, Bissell had decided to settle here. He assembled an estate of nearly 2,300 acres, which he called Franklinville Farm. He may have started his Federal-style house in 1812, and construction continued until about 1819, creating an unusual L-shaped floorplan with two lobbies. General Bissell returned here in 1821 when he retired. About 1890 his grandson replaced the old stone kitchen with a two-story frame wing.

Five generations of Bissells resided here. Great-granddaughter Janet Bissell Dimond gave the nine remaining acres to the county between 1960 and 1964. Architect Gerhardt Kramer then restored the house, which was furnished with the assistance of St. Louis County Historic Buildings Commission member Carolyn McDonnell. It now reflects life during the first three generations of Bissells. The house was listed in the National Register of Historic Places in 1978.

County Parks now also owns the site of Fort Belle Fontaine overlooking the Missouri River at the mouth of Coldwater Creek, a park with outstanding scenic value as well as historic interest. Fort Belle Fontaine was established in 1805 as the first US military installation west of the Mississippi River. The Lewis and Clark expedition camped here in 1806 on the last night of their epic journey, and the National Park Service has erected signs in the park commemorating that event. General Bissell moved the fort from the bank of the river to the top of the bluff after 1808. With the departure of the army for Jefferson Barracks in 1826, the fort disappeared.

The city of St. Louis acquired the site in 1913 for a juvenile rehabilitation facility called Bellefontaine Farm, later the Missouri Hills Home for Boys. The city developed the area along the river for use as a city park in the late 1930s, using WPA funds. This was part of the same effort that developed Tilles Park. Some remains are still visible, notably the monumental stone staircase descending from the bluff to the river.

The city sold a large portion of the Missouri Hills Home to the county in 1985, retaining the juvenile home buildings at the center of the site. The state of Missouri acquired that core in 1988, and the Division of Youth Services now operates it as the Fort Bellefontaine Campus.

Founded
1963

Size
1,583.06 Acres

GREENSFELDER PARK

Courtesy of Steve Tiemann

Greensfelder Park forms the heart of a West County greenbelt that includes Camp Wyman, the Missouri Conservation Department's Rockwood Reservation and Rockwood Range, and Babler State Park. Much of this land was first assembled in the 1850s by William T. Christy and Robert K. Woods of Woods, Christy & Co., a dry goods company in downtown St. Louis. Woods and Christy formed a lumber company that logged the area. The property later passed to Christy's son Calvin M. Christy, who extracted the clay and other minerals on the property for his Christy Fire Clay Company, organized in 1881. Christy sold to Charles Evans in 1893, and Evans is said to have offered a 300-acre tract to the city of St. Louis for use as a park. To enhance the site, a dam was constructed in 1895 on the property's main tributary, but it washed away during the spring rains of 1896.

Mining continued on the property under the Cobb, Wright and Case Mining Company, which went bankrupt in 1938. Missouri's Conservation Commission then acquired part of the former Christy property for Rockwoods Reservation but omitted the park's later site. It suffered from periodic logging operations, intense grazing from the nearby Allenton stockyards, and fire. The last severe forest fire occurred on Easter Sunday 1941.

The trustees of the St. Louis Regional Planning and Construction Foundation donated the park to St. Louis County in 1963. The foundation had been established in 1939 by A. P. Greensfelder (1879–1955), civic leader and chairman of the board of the Fruin-Colnon Construction Company. Albert Preston Greensfelder had been the primary force behind the creation of Creve Coeur Lake Park and became chairman of the county's first Parks Advisory Board. He intended the foundation to provide financial assistance to public improvements, civic projects, and engineering programs, especially education and research.

Courtesy of Steve Tiemann

Originally called Rockwood Park, the park was officially renamed in September 1965. The first phase of construction began the next year. Another major development, involving picnic areas, the visitor center, the equestrian areas, and a new barn, was dedicated in 1973. The Muckerman Shelter was completed in November 1981. In 1994, Sonya Glassberg dedicated the Myron Glassberg Pavilion in memory of her husband, who had been the nephew and ward of Mr. Greensfelder's wife, Blanche. The pavilion replaced a family picnic shelter that had formerly been in the park.

The County's long association with Wyman Center was strengthened in 2021 when 157 acres of Camp Wyman were transferred to the adjacent park.

Founded 1950

Size 424.95 Acres

JEFFERSON BARRACKS PARK

Courtesy of Steve Tiemann

The US War Department acquired the 1,700-acre Jefferson Barracks Military Reservation in 1826 and deactivated the army post in 1946. The Veterans Hospital and National Cemetery still occupy parts of the site, while the main parade ground with its historic buildings from the 1890s is controlled by the National Guard. The oldest surviving buildings date to the 1850s and are found in the northernmost 425 acres, now Jefferson Barracks Park, while the most historic landscape is protected by the smaller Sylvan Springs Park. The county acquired both from the General Services Administration immediately after the Parks Department was created in 1950.

Jefferson Barracks was founded six days after the death of Thomas Jefferson and in the following decades became an important staging center during wars and operations in the West. More than 200 men who became Union and Confederate generals served here before the Civil War, including Grant and Lee. During that war, vast temporary hospitals at Jefferson Barracks treated the wounded from both sides. Park historian Marc Kollbaum has been telling this important story in his series of books, *Gateway to the West: The History of Jefferson Barracks*, for sale through the Friends of Jefferson Barracks.

In 1850, the St. Louis Arsenal opened a branch at the Barracks, intended to reduce the risk of explosion at its base in the Soulard neighborhood. The stone Laborer's House and Old Ordnance Room were built the following year, and the sturdy Powder Magazine followed in 1857. The county opened the Powder Magazine Museum in 1960 to document the history of the Barracks. The Old Ordnance Room houses changing exhibitions. Through the efforts of the Friends of Jefferson Barracks, the 1870 barn was restored and reconstructed in 2003 as a visitors and education center, including a shop. The park also features the Veterans Memorial, an amphitheater designed in 1990 by Team Four Architects. The 3-mile Dennis Schick Trail opened in 1995.

The Missouri Civil War Museum and the Southwestern Bell Pioneers have restored buildings facing the parade ground, and a museum dedicated to prisoners of war and those missing in action (POW-MIA) is planned.

Sylvan Springs Park was created by the army, beginning in 1939, when the 6th Infantry created a stone "beverage garden" around the springs. The USO hosted many shows there during World War II, with major entertainers such as Jeanette MacDonald and Judy Garland. After 1954, Sylvan Springs drew crowds with carnival rides in the spring. A skateboard park opened in 2007, designed by staff landscape architect Chris Ludwig and skateboarders themselves. The south half of the park was transferred to the National Cemetery in 2024.

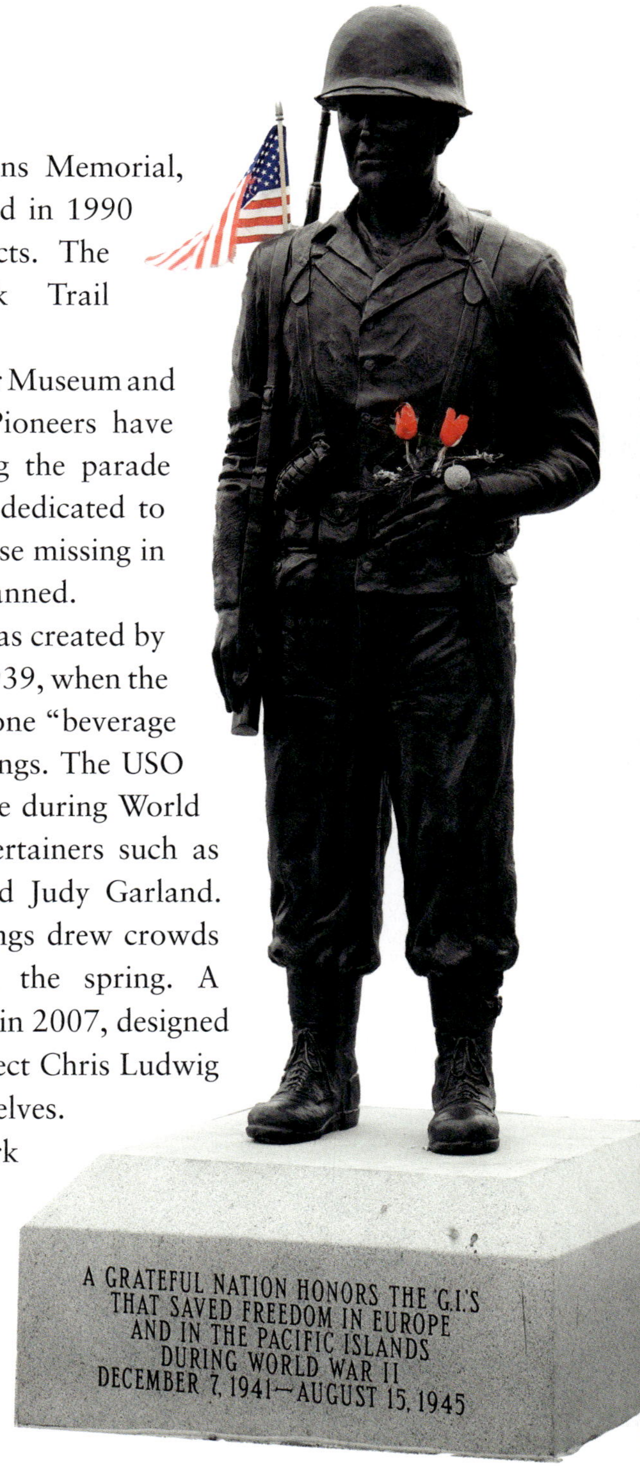

Courtesy of Steve Tiemann

Courtesy of Steve Tiemann

Images courtesy of Steve Tiemann

Founded	Size
1968	94.16 Acres

LAUMEIER SCULPTURE PARK

Courtesy of Steve Tiemann

Now a sculpture park with a national reputation, Henry H. Laumeier Park was originally a country estate, one of a group of such estates created by business leaders, mostly of German origin, moving out along Watson and Gravois Roads from the Compton Heights neighborhood of South St. Louis. Roland L. Kahle built a house in 1917 on Rott Road next to his brother's new home. The Kahles Ringen Stove Company became part of the American Stove Company, maker of Magic Chef stoves. The architect, Ernst Janssen, was known for his large Compton Heights mansion. Here, he created a glorified stone bungalow with matching garage and gatehouse.

Henry H. Laumeier (1876–1959), a real estate investor from the same neighborhood as Kahle, purchased the estate in 1936. He married Matilda Cramer in 1941, and they expanded the Rott Road property to 72 acres. Matilda Laumeier met Wayne C. Kennedy, county parks director, in 1963 and discussed her desire for a park that would retain the landscape and not redevelop it with playing fields. She bequeathed the property to the county in 1968, including a gift of $25,000 toward the cost of development.

At first intended as a nature study center, Laumeier Park was transformed in 1975 by the offer made by St. Louis sculptor Ernest Trova to make a gift of 40 of his own sculptures as the nucleus of a sculpture park and gallery. At that time, only a few such parks existed in the world, and in this country only the Storm King Center in New York had a similar mission.

With the Trova gift installed, the park reopened in 1976. Over the years, many sculptures have been installed temporarily, from months to years, making the park a constantly changing spectacle. Some were greeted by the public with dismay at first, but over the years appreciation has grown, aided by the park's education program. Alexander Liberman's enormous metal abstraction,

Courtesy of Steve Tiemann

The Way, was once featured on the cover of the telephone book.

A group of friends purchased about 20 acres on the east boundary of the park in 1981 and held it for several years until the county could reimburse them. These woods have become the home for several large works commissioned specifically for the land from artists Jackie Ferrara, Mary Miss, Beverly Pepper, and others. Additionally, the Aaronson Fine Art Center, designed by Tivers Associates, opened in 2015, providing a new indoor gallery space and permitting the original house to become the Kranzberg Educational Lab. Another site-specific commission by Richard Fleischner crosses Rott Road to include stone constructions on the north side. Gallery exhibitions in the house are frequent, and special events such as the juried art fair held on Mother's Day weekend have become traditions.

Founded

1970

Size

569.47 Acres

QUEENY PARK

Courtesy of Steve Tiemann

Queeny Park was once part of the estate of the late Mr. and Mrs. Edgar M. Queeny. Edgar Queeny was the former president and chairman of the board of Monsanto Chemical Company, which was founded by his father. The history of the land, however, traces much further back than the Queenys.

The Jarville House is, after the Hanley House in Clayton, the most imposing example of the Greek Revival style to survive in St. Louis County, and its comparative modesty suggests the distinction between what was thought proper for city and country. St. Louis was at the time a stronghold of the Greek Revival, the surviving examples of which (the Courthouse, the old Cathedral, and the Chatillon-DeMenil House) only suggest the extent and splendor of the style as it was seen here. Jarville, at 1723 Mason Road, was built about 1854 by Hyacinth Renard. It was renovated by architect William Crowell of the firm of Mauran, Russell & Crowell following the Queenys' acquisition of it in 1931. The house was listed in the National Register of Historic Places in 1984. It currently houses the Museum of the Dog. A second historic house on the property is the Henry Weidman House off Weidman Road. It is customarily leased to park employees.

The Queenys sold their property to the American Investment Company Realty Corporation in 1964, giving the proceeds to Barnes Hospital. St. Louis County purchased the property from the American Investment Company in March 1970 for $3,310,000 from 1969 bond issue funds. Ethel Queeny contributed $1 million toward the completion of the family recreation complex. Edward Greensfelder, who represents the Albert P. Greensfelder Foundation, also donated $1 million for the project, along with an additional $50,000 for landscaping.

Courtesy of Steve Tiemann

Sverdrup and Parcel & Associates Inc. served as architect for Greensfelder Memorial Complex, which began construction in June 1972 and was dedicated in September 1974. The main building houses a regulation-size ice-skating rink, skate rental and sharpening, a concession area, and lockers. The main structure is also a multipurpose building with 22,500 square feet that can accommodate special events. The original tent structure—completed in August of 1978, designed by Jones/Mayer & Associates Inc.—covered 14,000 square feet. The tensile cover was designed and assembled by Birdair Structures Inc. of Buffalo, New York. In June 1994, the tent was replaced by a pre-engineered metal canopy. Funds were contributed from Midwest Sport Hockey Inc. and Perry Turnbull, a former St. Louis Blues hockey player. This facility was enclosed in 1998 with private funding.

Courtesy of Steve Tiemann

Courtesy of Steve Tiemann

Founded

1969

Size

241.64 Acres

SPANISH LAKE PARK

Courtesy of Steve Tiemann

Courtesy of Steve Tiemann

Along with Creve Coeur Lake, the county's first park, and Charbonier Bluff, which still remains in private ownership, Spanish Lake has the longest history as a natural feature admired for its scenic beauty and recreational potential. Unlike Creve Coeur Lake, Spanish Lake was created not by shifting river channels but by the geology of the region. Depressions or sinkholes are caused by the collapse of the underlying limestone from groundwater erosion. Most sinkholes drain naturally, but if they become plugged, a pond results. Sunfish Lake, the second lake in this park, appeared in just this way in July 1942 when Ben Ruthmann found that his tomato field had been inundated.

Spanish Lake has been known as a beauty spot since colonial times, but it remained in private ownership until St. Louis County acquired it in 1971 with a federal grant and funds from the 1969 bond issue.

In the 1770s, Spanish troops were reportedly stationed at the temporary fort near the mouth of the Missouri River. Zenon Trudeau, the lieutenant governor of Upper Missouri, also had a country retreat at the lake. Records from 1809 show that the first to legally claim the northwest part of the lake was John Lard, whose son was the first owner of the nearby Fort Belle Fontaine site. The southeast part of the lake was claimed by Jacques St. Vrain, who had already purchased the site from the widow Rigoche. Through the rest of that century the lake was owned by prominent nonresidents such as John O'Fallon, but in 1897 the Spanish Lake Park subdivision was platted by developers. Fortunately for posterity, it was not successful, but later subdivisions threatened the lake right up to the time the county intervened. Even today a significant tract of subdivided but undeveloped land remains immediately southeast of the park.

Since its opening, the park has received several improvements. Fourteen acres were added in 1986, and the large Manny Broadway Shelter was built at an elevated point on the east side of the lake. The lake was dredged in the 1990s and is now managed by the Missouri Department of Conservation under the Community Assistance Program. The Cardinal Care Program of the baseball Cardinals constructed Spirit Field, an accessible baseball field suitable for use by players in wheelchairs and others with disabilities.

Founded
1957

Size
75.45 Acres

TILLES PARK

Courtesy of Steve Tiemann

C. Andrew Tilles (1865–1951), called "Cap" by all, returned from Fort Smith, Arkansas, in 1876 to his native St. Louis, where he and his business partner Sam Adler parlayed a cigar store into the ownership of the South Side Race Track, later the site of McKinley High School. By 1906, Tilles, Adler, and Louis A. Cella were said to control more than half the racetracks in the country, including in Little Rock, Hot Springs, Memphis, Detroit, Cincinnati, and Louisville. When Missouri outlawed horse race betting that year, Tilles made even more by redeveloping his Delmar Race Track site in the present University City Loop.

Tilles acquired this park site in 1912 and created an estate he called Rest Haven. He deeded it in 1932 to the city of St. Louis, specifying that it be named Rosalie Tilles Children's Playground and Park in honor of his mother and that it be open to persons regardless of race or creed. He reserved his modest home and the surrounding 7.67 acres for his lifetime and that of his housekeeper, Jeanette Windegger. He gave another park to the city of Fort Smith in memory of his father.

Works Progress Administration (WPA) projects in 1936 and 1937 created the stone entrance pylons, picnic shelters, and comfort stations, all designed by Louis Baylor Pendleton (1875–1964). He moved the iron fence at the main entrance from Hyde Park in North St. Louis. Tilles Park remains one the finest New Deal projects in the county.

When the county bought the park in 1957, the city used the proceeds to create a new 29-acre Rosalie Tilles Park on Hampton Avenue at Fyler. After County Park Commissioner Charles Skow died in 1962, an attempt was made to rename the county park for him, but in the end a new picnic shelter sufficed. Another new shelter was named for Jeanette Windegger after she released her rights to the 7.67 acres in 1975. She devoted her remaining years to charitable works, dying in 1991 at the age of 97.

Courtesy of Steve Tiemann

The St. Louis Children's Hospital Accessible Playground opened in 2006. Designed by SWT Design with staff landscape architect Mike Flad, it accommodates children with an unusually wide range of disabilities and has become one of the most popular attractions in the park system. Another popular annual attraction is Winter Wonderland, which swathes the park in lights through the month of December.

Founded	Size
1968	199.34 Acres

BEE TREE PARK

Courtesy of Steve Tiemann

Courtesy of Steve Tiemann

Located near the far southeast corner of St. Louis County, with sweeping views of the Mississippi River, Bee Tree Park was once remote, but today development extends right up to the entrance. Bee Tree was originally created as a private estate by Eugene Nims (1865–1954), president of Southwestern Bell Telephone Company. Nims had started a telephone company in Oklahoma in 1896. Its 36 miles of wire eventually grew into Southwestern Bell. Nims became president in 1919 and built the Southwestern Bell Building at 1010 Pine Street in 1924. He and his wife, the unusually named Lotawana Flateau Nims (called "Miss Molly" by her friends), lived in Portland Place and had a summer home in Woods Hole, Massachusetts, but they added the magnificent Tudor Revival house at Bee Tree Farm to their collection in 1929 and used it as a weekend retreat. The house is characteristic of the picturesque and finely crafted designs of Maritz & Young, the foremost St. Louis residential architects of the era.

After Mrs. Nims died in 1966, development threatened the 192-acre site. The Open Space Foundation, led by Lindell Gordon and R. Walston Chubb, was able to raise $197,000, which matched federal funds to enable the county to purchase the property in 1968. Gordon, a trust officer of the Mississippi Valley Trust Company, was fatally ill at the time, and after his death the park created a garden and fountain in his memory. The fountain sculpture represents a gingko leaf and has the inscription, "The imprint of a dying leaf is wondrous to behold." It was created by Scopia, the partnership of sculptors Bill Severson and Saunders Schultz, while the garden was designed by the landscape architect Robert Goetz. The nearby overlook is dedicated to Chubb (1894–1977), a noted St. Louis attorney. The Chubb Pavilion, dedicated in 1981, was designed by landscape architect John Mareing and funded by friends of Walston Chubb.

The Golden Eagle River Museum occupied the Nims House from 1974 to 2004.

Founded

1954

Size

275.59 Acres

BUDER PARK

Courtesy of Steve Tiemann

Buder Park, like Tilles and Fort Belle Fontaine, was once part of a projected St. Louis City park system within the county. Gustavus A. Buder Sr. and his wife, Lydia, gave 70 acres to the city in 1917 and another 70 acres the following year, specifying that it be called Buder Bathing Beach and Recreation Camp. In accepting the property, Mayor Henry Kiel wrote, "You have given us the property, and if it is not developed the fault will be mine." Plans for rental cottages and boathouses were announced but never implemented.

Gustavus Buder was a lawyer and publisher of the *St. Louis Times* and the German-language *Westliche Post* until the early 1930s and had many other business interests. The Buder family supported the city in many ways, including donating the Buder Playground at Hickory Street and California Avenue, and added the Buder Recreation Center in 1930. The original Buder Branch Library opened in 1922. G. A. Buder Sr. died in 1954, and his will empowered his executors to recover the undeveloped park property from the city. They turned the land over to St. Louis County that same year.

The park's checkered history continued under the county. Over the years, the county has added more than 60 acres to the original Buder gift along the Meramec River and to the south. On the other hand, I-44 divided the Buder tract into two parts. The southern portion, at the top of the Meramec Valley bluff, has become known as Upper Buder. It has picnic shelters and tennis courts. Lower Buder, because of its level, unobstructed ground, has attracted a variety of special events over the years, including steeplechase horse racing.

Images courtesy of Mark Groth

Founded

1972

Size

525.86 Acres

CLIFF CAVE PARK

Courtesy of Steve Tiemann

Cliff Cave County Park
Courtesy of Steve Tiemann

The cave for which this park is named has been a landmark in southern St. Louis County since the original settlement of the area, marked "Indian Cave" on 19th-century maps. The mouth of the cave opens directly out of the Mississippi River bluff about 50 feet high and was described in 1895 as being "like the door of some ancient cathedral." The land around it, however, remains nearly as it was in the 1840s. Speculators tried unsuccessfully to develop a subdivision called Cave Cliffs as early as 1857. A decade later, a dentist named Christopher W. Spalding organized the Cliff Cave Wine Company. He planted about 25 acres of vines and built a wall across the face of the cave to use it as a cool storage room. During this time, the Indian Cave became a popular destination for steamboat excursions. The City of Alton advertised in 1876, "Get on board and get out of the heat and dust of the city for one day at least." The Iron Mountain Railroad erected a station at the foot of the bluff.

The wine failed to make a profit, and the Pettus family acquired the property in 1877. They held it for nearly a century until the county purchased the land in 1972, using proceeds from the 1969 bond issue and federal matching funds.

At first the cave was open to spelunkers in good weather, but it was permanently closed after six people tragically drowned during one of the record rainfalls of 1993. The flood that year also damaged the low land between the railroad line and the river. It was subsequently elevated using fill provided by the nearby Bussen Quarry. Twin Hollow Associates donated 239 acres of riverside land south of the park to the county in 2003, and it was subsequently paved with 3 miles of trails.

Founded
2001

Size
10.46 Acres

EBSWORTH PARK

Courtesy of Steve Tiemann

Even in a park system that includes a transportation museum and a sculpture park, a park that includes a house designed by the great American architect Frank Lloyd Wright has to stand out as unusual. The park is named for Alec W. and Bernice W. Ebsworth, the parents of Barney A. Ebsworth, a St. Louis businessman and nationally known collector of American art. He gave more than half of the $1.7 million raised to purchase the property from Russell Kraus, the original owner. The Frank Lloyd Wright House in Ebsworth Park is one of only five buildings in Missouri designed by Wright (1867–1959). It is a Usonian house, the term Wright used for his smaller houses for people of modest means, but it is also one of his most complex designs, based on two overlapping parallelograms of 60 and 120 degrees. Wright designed all the furnishings, which still exist, including parallelogram beds and special studio equipment for Kraus, an artist and graphic designer. Russell and his wife, Ruth, started building in 1951, moved in at the beginning of 1956, and continued work on the interiors until 1962. Kraus designed the striking leaded glass doors, the latest example of art glass in any Wright house. The property was listed in the National Register of Historic Places in 1997 as the Russell and Ruth Goetz Kraus House.

Starting in 1995, Judy Bettendorf and others created a 501(c)3 organization, later headed by Joanne Kohn, which raised the funds for purchase, restoration, and management. The county took the title on January 18, 2001, and immediately leased the property back to the organization. Architect John Eifler, of Eifler & Associates of Chicago, supervised restoration of the house. The organization has continued to make improvements to the property, including paving the gravel entrance drive. Volunteer docents lead tours by appointment.

Courtesy of Steve Tiemann

Founded	Size
1972	563.05 Acres

WAYNE C. KENNEDY PARK

Courtesy of Steve Tiemann

Courtesy of Steve Tiemann

Originally called South County Park, Kennedy was acquired and developed as one of three regional parks as a result of the $25 million bond issue passed by county voters in 1969. The others are Queeny Park to the west and Veterans Memorial Park to the north. The large recreation complex at the center of the park was designed by R. W. Booker & Associates.

The history of the land goes back to a 340-acre Spanish land grant, later confirmed by the US government as Survey 993. Taken together, Kennedy Park and the adjacent Lower Meramec Park constitute the whole grant, perhaps the only such grant in St. Louis County to remain largely devoted to open space and in a single ownership. (A runner-up would be Survey 2507, now divided between Glen Echo Country Club and St. Vincent Park.)

The park was renamed in 1993 in honor of Wayne C. Kennedy. Originally a teacher and assistant principal with the Mehlville School District, Kennedy joined the county's Department of Parks and Recreation in 1961. Just a year later he was named director of the department, and he served until 1991. In his three decades with the county, he was able to increase park acreage from just over 1,000 to nearly 13,000.

In addition to the Kennedy Recreation Complex, the park includes the Quail Creek Golf Course, which opened in 1987. A new playground was completed in 2002, and lighted tennis courts and picnic sites are also available.

Courtesy of Steve Tiemann

Founded
1964

Size
547.77 Acres

LONE ELK PARK

Courtesy of Steve Tiemann

Courtesy of Steve Tiemann

Along with West Tyson Park, Lone Elk is a remnant of the 2,400-acre Tyson Valley Powder Plant used for the testing and storage of ammunition during World War II. After the war, the whole tract was transferred to St. Louis County for use as a county park, and in 1948 herds of elk and bison were established there. Just a short time later, however, the land was reacquired by the federal government at the onset of the Korean conflict, and for safety reasons the wildlife herds were destroyed in 1958. One lone bull elk somehow survived.

Many people assumed that the Tyson Valley site would eventually be returned to the county. But when the opportunity arose, Washington University made a counter proposal that carried the day. Through the efforts of Parks Director Wayne Kennedy, however, the county was able to reacquire 405 acres of the original tract in 1964 for $60,787. The name was changed in 1966 from Tyson Park to Lone Elk Park. Six additional elk were obtained from Yellowstone National Park that year through the efforts of the children of the Rockwood School District and West St. Louis County Lions Club. Six bison were acquired from the Saint Louis Zoo in July 1973. Both the elk and the bison have gradually increased to substantial herds.

The World Bird Sanctuary, formerly the Raptor Rehabilitation and Propagation Project, occupied the visitor center at Lone Elk from 1986 to 2003. Since then it has been situated on its own 305-acre site across Lone Elk Park Road from the main park entrance.

Courtesy of Steve Tiemann

Founded 1978

Size 132.39 Acres

ST. VINCENT PARK

Courtesy of Steve Tiemann

Courtesy of Steve Tiemann

The magnificent Châteauesque building at the heart of St. Vincent Park is the former St. Vincent Hospital, built between 1892 and 1895 by the Daughters of Charity of St. Vincent de Paul to relocate their mental facility from the Soulard neighborhood. The architect was George R. Mann, who was working on the St. Louis City Hall at the same time, but the design was probably by Mann's employee Harvey Ellis, a celebrated talent of the time. The grounds around the hospital were used until the late 1940s by the nuns and patients to raise crops and graze cows and hogs for food.

The Daughters of Charity established their provincial house in 1914 on land north of the "Castle." The cemetery for the order opened in 1928, and Marillac College operated still further north from 1955 to 1974. The college and provincial house have been acquired by the University of Missouri–St. Louis. The hospital closed in June 1978, and the Daughters of Charity relocated their medical activities to the DePaul Community Health Center.

At that time, St. Louis County purchased the land around the hospital, supported by grants from the National Park Service. The Castle was not included in the park but was renovated as Castle Park Apartments. It was listed in the National Register of Historic Places in 1982.

The St. Vincent Community Center was opened in June 1989 as a result of the 1986 voter-approved bond issue monies. It has space for recreation programs, civic group meetings, and organized basketball and day camps at the facility. The water park was opened in 1994 with a water slide and 80-foot flume ride. The playground was redeveloped in 2001. Acquisition of a small parcel on the east side of Salerno Drive in 2003 has permitted creation of a loop trail around the Castle.

Park	Founded	Size
Sioux Passage	1965	211.6 Acres
John D. Briscoe	2002	37.68 Acres

SIOUX PASSAGE PARK

Courtesy of Steve Tiemann

The land that has become Sioux Passage Park was purchased in 1965 with money from a bond issue, but its history goes back to the Late Woodland and Mississippian periods. Sioux Passage Park Archaeological Site was listed in the National Register of Historic Places in 1974.

The park is one of few places in the county with a wide public access to the Missouri River. Early explorers passed here, and the journal of Zebulon Pike refers to camping in this vicinity. Steamboats began to ply the river in the 1820s, and one of them, the *Car of Commerce*, foundered and sank near here in 1832, giving its name to the passage of the river called the Car of Commerce Chute.

Beyond the chute is Pelican Island, a tract of nearly 2,000 acres given to St. Louis County by Joseph Desloge and deeded by the county to the Missouri Department of Conservation in 1991 but never officially opened to the public.

John D. Briscoe Park is a tract of 33 acres adjacent to the entrance to Sioux Passage Park on Old Jamestown Road and almost indistinguishable from it. John Briscoe bequeathed the property to the county as an act of civic generosity in 2002. The land had been farmed by Mrs. Briscoe's grandfather and other members of the family for a century, but it is now being returned to a natural condition.

Courtesy of Steve Tiemann

Founded

1962

Size

97.44 Acres

SUSON PARK

Courtesy of Steve Tiemann

Courtesy of Steve Tiemann

The original Suson tract was purchased by the county from Sidney Salomon Jr. in 1962. He was a well-known figure in St. Louis at the time as owner of the old Sportsman's Park. His fame increased in 1966 when he acquired the Arena and became the first owner of the St. Louis Blues hockey team. The name of this park originated with Salomon as a combination of his children's names, Susan and Sonny.

Suson Park was intended to be a farm park from the outset, and because several of the buildings and the five lakes were already in existence when the land was purchased, both the animal farm and the lake fishing attractions were available when the park opened in 1964. The large new barn was constructed with funds from the 1969 bond issue. County Parks dredged the largest lake in 1978, creating a new depth of 10 feet from the original one to three feet. The Missouri Department of Conservation stocks this lake. O'Fallon Brothers Construction Company deeded 10 more acres to the park in 1980.

Suson Park draws its land from several different 19th-century farms, but the main part of the park belonged to Frederick Hagemann, who sold it to Julius Riepe in about 1872. Riepe built the old brick house at the center of the park, now painted white with many later additions.

Most types of animals typical to Missouri farms can be seen at Suson, including draft horses and dairy cattle.

Founded
1970

Size
243.23 Acres

VETERANS MEMORIAL PARK

Courtesy of Steve Tiemann

Like Queeny and Wayne C. Kennedy Parks, Veterans Memorial Park resulted from the passage by the voters of a $25 million bond issue in 1969. The county bought 227.4 acres of the present park the next year. The recreation complex was constructed in 1976, designed by the architectural firm Hastings & Chivetta. The building was substantially renovated from 2009 to 2011, when the indoor skating rink was replaced by a multipurpose gymnasium.

The present park constitutes almost 40 percent of a historic mile-square (640-acre) tract known as Survey 2495, claimed by William Robertson, a farmer from New Madrid County, as compensation for damages sustained in the great New Madrid earthquakes of 1811 and 1812. Redman Road, named for local farmer C. B. Redman, follows the southern boundary of the survey, and Parker Road follows the northern boundary.

The idea of a golf course at Veterans Park was broached as early as 1973, and construction specifications were drawn up in 1977 by David Gill, a golf course architect. The present Eagle Springs Golf Course was not authorized by the County Council until 1986, however.

Courtesy of Steve Tiemann

MORE COUNTY PARKS

West Tyson Chubb Trail
Courtesy of Steve Tiemann

In addition to the 22 parks already described, St. Louis County's park system includes the following 23 parks in active use. At least that many more sites are undeveloped, awaiting future planning or leased to other entities, public and private. The geographical and functional range of these parks reflects the dual nature of the county system, serving both as a regional park system and, in lieu of a municipal park system, for the unincorporated county, providing smaller neighborhood parks and playgrounds, particularly in the north and south regions. As parts of the county have incorporated, at least 18 additional parks have been transferred by the county to other agencies.

NORTH

Bella Fontaine Park	209.93 acres
Bon Oak Park	15.31 acres
Castlepoint Park	10.78 acres
Norman B. Champ Park	101.38 acres
Endicott Park	24.04 acres
Martin Luther King Jr. Memorial Park	4.01 acres
Kinloch Park	9.23 acres
Larimore Park	24.54 acres
James S. McDonnell Memorial Park	133.21 acres

WEST

John Allen Love Park	89.03 acres
Memorial Park	2.68 acres
Ohlendorf West Park	46.07 acres
West Tyson Park	672.57 acres

SOUTH

Affton White-Rodgers Community Center	7.98 acres
Black Forest Park	4.25 acres
Bohrer Park	16.48 acres
Blake C. Snyder Memorial Park (formerly Clydesdale Park)	117.96 acres
Lemay Park	18.46 acres
Mathilda-Welmering Park	6.19 acres
Ohlendorf Park	10.03 acres
Henry L. Simpson Park	175 acres
Unger Park	94.85 acres
George Winter Park	159.73 acres

MUNICIPAL PARKS

Courtesy of Steve Tiemann

Almost 40 of St. Louis County's 91 cities and villages maintain at least one park or playground. Some of these municipal parks predate the county's park system. In University City, for example, voters established a park board in 1922 and the following year approved a bond issue that paid for five parks, including the 93-acre Heman Park. Since then, University City has established a park to honor each of its outgoing mayors. The city of Clayton acquired 51 acres in 1935 and developed it with WPA grants, naming it Shaw Park for its mayor at the time.

The majority of municipal parks are neighborhood playgrounds. Ten of these were originally created by County Parks and subsequently transferred to a locality, such as Tanglewood Park in Bellefontaine Neighbors and Vinita County Park, the namesake for the Vinita Park neighborhood. Only a few municipal parks approach a hundred acres. Bluebird Park in Ellisville has 167.36 acres, but that includes the 67.42-acre Klamberg Woods, which is actually owned by the Conservation Department. Kirkwood Park extends to 92 acres and Florissant's Sunset Park to 90 acres.

Most municipal parks have been paid for by tax revenues, and St. Louis County voters have a proud record of supporting parks at the polls. One notable example is Wild Acres Park in Overland, 31.25 acres at Midland and Ashby, rescued from development by the citizens in 1995. Several of the larger cities have invested substantially in recreation complexes, which are seen as enhancing the desirability of the community and giving it a special identity. Another source of community identity has been the preservation of historic houses in parks. The Payne-Gentry House in Bridgeton, Hanley House in Clayton, Sappington House in Crestwood, and Hawken House in Webster Groves are all located in city parks. Black Jack and Crestwood are notable among cities that also maintain historic cemeteries, both for their scenic beauty and their historic significance.

MUNICIPALITIES MAINTAINING PARKS

Ballwin
Bellefontaine Neighbors
Bel Ridge
Berkeley
Black Jack
Breckenridge Hills
Brentwood
Bridgeton
Chesterfield
Clayton
Country Club Hills
Crestwood
Creve Coeur
Dellwood
Des Peres
Edmundson
Ellisville
Eureka
Fenton
Ferguson
Florissant
Hazelwood
Jennings
Kirkwood
Manchester
Maplewood
Maryland Heights
Normandy
Northwoods
Olivette
Overland
Riverview
St. Ann
St. George
Shrewsbury
Sunset Hills
University City
Vinita Park
Webster Groves

STATE PARKS

NiNi Harris

Castlewood State Park
Courtesy of Steve Tiemann

The music of songbirds, the buzzing of insects, and the sounds of rippling waters fill the air of the Missouri State Parks that circle St. Louis. Their rugged trails weave paths through fallen trees coated with thick green moss, wildflowers that pop up in spring, and carpets of rust-colored leaves in fall. The forest undergrowth brushes against the legs of hikers as they follow these paths under the canopy of oak, hickory, and conifer forests.

The parks provide intimate, wild settings hidden in the woods or breathtaking panoramas of the tree-covered, rolling landscape of the Ozark foothills. St. Louisans see limestone bluffs that tower over the Meramec River or the awe-inspiring confluence of the Mississippi and Missouri Rivers in nearby state parks. While some parks offer museums, equestrian trails, and camping facilities, others only allow day visitors walking the trails. Each, however, preserves and restores natural environments while providing St. Louisans with ways to relish the region's natural beauty while staying close to home.

Spirited St. Louisans and the organizations they formed spurred the creation of the state parks on the periphery of St. Louis. Jacob and Henry Babler donated and endowed the land for Babler State Park in honor of their brother, a St. Louis physician. Four housewives in Jefferson County rallied support and raised $568,000 to save Mastodon State Historic Site (originally a state park) from developers. An entrepreneur who hawked his spot remover on late-night television commercials purchased and gave the people of Missouri Don Robinson State Park.

The Open Space Foundation of St. Louis, founded in 1965 to serve as a steward of nature, was key to establishing Castlewood State Park. This was only part of their massive effort to restore and support a clean and healthy Meramec River watershed. The Danforth Foundation, established by Ralston Purina founder William Danforth in 1927, made possible the initial purchase of land at the confluence of the Mississippi and Missouri Rivers. Edward "Ted" Jones and his wife, Pat Jones, were dedicated to state conservation efforts.

Castlewood State Park
Courtesy of Steve Tiemann

The Missouri State Parks responded to these generous St. Louisans by helping ring St. Louis with parks. In 1917, inspired by the creation of the National Parks Service, Missouri funded the park system using revenue from the fish and game department. Taking leadership from the National Park Service, the Missouri State Parks put young men with the Civilian Conservation Corps to work building trails, picnic shelters, cabins, and stone bridges in a distinctive, rustic style.

Under the leadership of the Missouri Department of Natural Resources since 1974, the system has grown with the creation of Castlewood, Confluence Point, and Route 66 State Parks. These parks—lands that were reclaimed for nature—now offer St. Louisans nature's gifts.

Founded	Size	Cost
1938	2,441 Acres	Donated

DR. EDMUND A. BABLER MEMORIAL STATE PARK

Courtesy of Steve Tiemann

Along with the overpowering statue of Dr. Edmund Babler, a life-size statue in the park honors the laborers with the CCC who developed this park and countless other parks across the nation.

The hundreds of natural acres of Babler State Park were celebrated as "the finest bit of old Missouri left untouched" when the land was donated for the park in 1934. The *Globe-Democrat* declared, "There you see the woods as they were in Laclede's and Chouteau's day." The sensations of walking along Babler Park's leaf-covered paths, with autumn sunlight showering through naked branches, continue to offer a primeval forest experience.

Miles of trails—enclosed by forests, following crooked creek beds and running along rock outcroppings that seem to weep water after rains—offer intimate, peaceful settings disrupted only by the rustling of squirrels in the leaves. The paths, rough-cut stone bridges, and rustic buildings of stone and heavy timbers seem to melt into the natural landscape.

The entrance to Babler, in contrast to the rest of the park, forms a dramatic, sweeping landscape. Wing walls of giant stone flank the wide road entering the park. Near this gate, an expansive lawn provides the setting for the statue of Dr. Edmund Babler, for whom the park is named. Prominent New York–based sculptor Charles Keck created the powerful statue, a bronze figure of Babler atop a granite pedestal.

The surprising main entrance to the park and statue of Babler remind visitors of the era when the park was founded—the Great Depression. Hardship gripped crowded urban neighborhoods and ecological disasters left farmers with barren fields and dust storms. In these harsh times, Jacob and Henry Babler donated the natural acreage on the outskirts of St. Louis County to provide a retreat for St. Louis residents. The gift was made in honor of their brother, Dr. Edmund A. Babler, a St. Louis physician and surgeon known for his generous spirit. Between 1934 and 1936, the brothers added more land to their initial gift of 868 acres of Ozarks foothills.

The gate, the miles of trails, the buildings of stone quarried on-site, and the timber picnic shelter with a stone fireplace at its center were all the work of members of the Civilian Conservation Corps (CCC). The CCC was one of President Franklin D. Roosevelt's programs created to address the massive unemployment of the Great Depression by putting young men to work on reforestation, erosion control, and the development of state and national parks. Two CCC camps were established in Babler with the mission of making the park accessible without detracting from its natural character. The young men with the CCC cut trails through the rugged landscape, constructed the pavilions, and built curving roadways. They built according to the philosophy of the National Park System of creating structures that fit each park's history and setting.

While most of the state parkland near St. Louis had to be reclaimed by nature, thanks to the vision of the Babler Family, Babler State Park's land was kept pristine.

Courtesy of Steve Tiemann

Founded	Size	Cost
1974	1,819 Acres	Donated by Open Space STL

CASTLEWOOD STATE PARK

The World Bird Sanctuary, located on land leased from the park, houses live birds that were injured and are unable to return to the wild. The sanctuary also features interpretive displays on birds of prey.

Courtesy of Steve Tiemann

Castlewood Park straddles the Meramec River, which twists south, east, north, and east again creating dramatic scenes with 200-foot-tall limestone bluffs and peaceful vistas with sandy beaches. Spring torrents eat away at the muddy banks of the Meramec, turning them into curving walls of earth edging the channel. Patches of bluebells seem to decorate the bottomland along the river in spring. The retreating waters of dry summer months reveal beds of gravel or wide beaches.

Twenty miles of trails explore this rugged landscape. The trails follow the bluffs or riverbanks or lead into the upland forests of white oak, northern red oak, and shagbark hickory. The forest is dense with thick underbrush and fallen tree trunks, their bark peeling.

Concrete and stone ruins peeking out through the beds of fallen leaves are a memory from the 1920s and 1930s. At that time this acreage along the Meramec was a resort with clubhouses and hotels, including one hotel that boasted 40 rooms. These buildings catered to St. Louisans escaping the summer heat. They took a Saturday commuter train to the cool valley of the Meramec River. As many as 10,000 people would descend on the beach or paddle the river in canoes. Young men romanced young ladies by playing the ukelele. On Saturday nights, the young St. Louisans put on skits in the clubhouses or danced till dawn.

Following World War II, increased auto ownership enabled St. Louisans to travel further in search of other rural retreats. Cabins to hotels along the Meramec were abandoned or burned. The Meramec's riverbanks became dumping grounds for old refrigerators and stoves, scarring the area's natural beauty.

An even bigger battle was escalating over the future of the Meramec, which wanders 218 miles from its Missouri headwaters to its mouth emptying into the Mississippi. Its basin drains almost 4,000 square miles of Missouri. A proposal to dam the river persisted. The dam would have flooded the valley, creating a huge resort lake. Recreational boaters supported the dam.

Courtesy of Steve Tiemann

The emerging environmental movement fought it, spreading awareness of the threat the dam posed to the ecosystem.

With the heated debate over the proposed dam as the backdrop, the Open Space Council (now known as Open Space STL) made two separate land acquisitions, then donated them for a state park. Castlewood State Park, framing miles of the banks of the Meramec, was established in 1974.

The following year, then–Governor Christopher S. Bond designated the 108-mile stretch of the river from Meramec State Park to the Mississippi River as the Meramec River Recreation Area. The corridor forms a greenway of unlinked parks and open spaces.

In a referendum on August 8, 1978, voters in the St. Louis area and in 10 rural counties of the Meramec basin rejected the dam by a vote of almost two to one.

After surviving threats to its ecosystem and natural beauty, Castlewood State Park is an inspiration. It is again rugged and lush and is treasured by St. Louisans.

Courtesy of Steve Tiemann

Courtesy of Steve Tiemann

Founded	Size	Cost
1976	418 Acres	Donated

MASTODON STATE HISTORIC SITE

Clovis Point refers to stone, spearhead-shaped projectiles with sharp edges that were attached to a stick or wooden shaft to be used as a spear, atlatl, or other hunting weapon by early man in North America. These stone projectile points were named after Clovis, New Mexico, where the examples were first found.

Courtesy of Steve Tiemann

Mastodon State Historic Site
Courtesy of Steve Tiemann

For almost two centuries, this primitive woodland site has lured visitors with its mysterious remnants from prehistoric times. Through the decades, hucksters, souvenir hunters, quarries, and finally developers threatened to erase its mysterious past before it was fully appreciated. Then, in the 1970s, four Jefferson County housewives saved the "bone bed" and surrounding 418 acres as a site of the Missouri Department of Natural Resources. Today Mastodon State Historic Site boasts trails, a bird habitat, and a museum of its natural history.

In 1839, a private entrepreneur and St. Louis Museum owner, Albert C. Koch, investigated a report of bones weathering out of banks along Rock Creek, then known as Sulphur Springs. This first-known study of the site revealed fossils later determined to be mastodon bones. At the turn of the century, amateur St. Louis paleontologist C. W. Beehler excavated skulls, jaws, giant tusks, and other fossils at the bone bed. His shack-like museum became a destination for railroad tours from St. Louis and a side trip for visitors attending the World's Fair in 1904. Interest in the bone bed was revived by the work of an archaeologist with the Works Progress Administration, and other private excavations were made.

A picture emerged of the area at the end of the last ice age (35,000 to 10,000 years ago). The remains suggested that when the glaciers to the north were slowly melting as the earth warmed, the area was swampy and contained mineral springs. It attracted giant ground sloths along with elephant-like mastodons with seven-foot-long tusks. These animals became trapped in the mud, where their bones were fossilized. The Ohio Sand Mine Co. owned and quarried the land without concern for the relics. They burned ancient bones in their lime kiln.

The Missouri Highway Department acquired the land during the planning of nearby I-55. During the 1970s, the department intended to sell the current park site, with its bone bed, to a developer. Four Jefferson County housewives

Courtesy of Steve Tiemann

Courtesy of Steve Tiemann

(Dorothy Heinze, who lived all her life within a mile from the bone bed; Marilyn King; Rita Naes; and Hazel Lee) organized the Mastodon Park Committee and rallied everyone from school children to office holders to the cause. The highway department gave the committee 13 months to raise $568,000 for the land; otherwise it would be sold for development.

The 418-acre park was established in 1976, and the committee's efforts were more than justified three years later when a paleontologist at Mastodon found a Clovis Point (an early spear head). This find established that the Missouri bone bed was the site of Clovis man (an early ancestor of Native Americans). Further findings at the bone bed indicated Clovis Man and mastodons overlapped in time at this site, and even suggested that Clovis Man was hunting mastodons.

The story of the bone bed, the mastodons, the Clovis point, and the receding glaciers is told through a life-size diorama in the site's museum.

With its walls built of stone quarried nearby, the museum built in the 1980s seems to melt into the landscape. Wilson-Jones, Inc. of Clayton designed the building to fit the slope of the landscape with its rock outcroppings. One hundred steps descend under a tree-canopied trail from the museum to the bone bed.

Courtesy of Steve Tiemann

Founded
1999

Size
409 Acres

ROUTE 66 STATE PARK

Courtesy of Steve Tiemann

With the creation of Route 66 State Park, another link was formed in the green corridor of parks and natural areas along the Meramec. Visitors walking easy trails or picnicking by the meandering Meramec River enjoy the final incarnation of this site that was once a town, then became a ghost town, and was then reclaimed from notorious contamination. The park site, once a dangerous eyesore, is now an asset.

Development of this site began in 1925, when a daily newspaper, the *St. Louis Times*, conducted a promotion for subscriptions in combination with the development of this site as a resort. The *Times* offered lots measuring 20 feet by 100 feet for only $67.50 with a six-month subscription to the paper. This working-class resort with swimming, fishing, and boating was named for the newspaper, Times Beach.

When the national economy plummeted following the stock market crash of 1929, demand for weekend homes disappeared. Instead, the people built humble homes on inexpensive lots and Times Beach evolved as a town. Route 66 was extended near Times Beach by the construction of the Meramec River Bridge, which opened in 1932. A few years later, a large, rambling frame roadhouse was built at the entrance to the Bridge. The Bridgehead Inn catered to the growing traffic on Route 66.

Times Beach was incorporated in 1957 and grew to about 2,000 residents. The working-class community, however, could not afford to pave its streets. The community addressed the clouds of dust created by each passing car by hiring a waste hauler to spray the roads of Times Beach with a dust suppressant. The contract lasted four years. The residents of Times Beach had no idea that the hauler sprayed a mixture laced with dioxin, a highly toxic chemical compound, on the streets, contaminating the town.

Courtesy of Steve Tiemann

When the consequences of the dioxin spray were discovered, the EPA conducted a soil sample study. The dangerous level of dioxin along the roads was reported on December 4, 1982. The following day, the Meramec River overflowed its banks and flooded Times Beach, spreading the contamination. The plight of an entire community, exiled at Christmastime, captured headlines.

Times Beach was permanently evacuated. Eventually the federal and state governments bought out the properties.

The speed of the land's recovery was as remarkable as the contamination was disturbing. The vacant buildings were mowed down and the polluted ground incinerated. The Parks Department planted native trees. Through the years, the trees began to cover the street lanes in the empty community. Health was restored to the acreage sandwiched between the railroad tracks, the old Route 66 and the banks of the Meramec.

In 1999, the state opened the former resort land as the Route 66 State Park. Bicyclers as well as people in wheelchairs enjoy the accessible trails through the park and the views of the Meramec River. Each year thousands of travelers following the 2,400-mile route of the old Route 66 stop in this park to view the Meramec and the skeleton of the old Meramec River Bridge. They visit the old Bridgehead Inn, which has been converted into a visitor center recalling the heyday of Route 66. A plaque comemorates the story of the environmental disaster at Times Beach.

Courtesy of Steve Tiemann

Courtesy of Steve Tiemann

Courtesy of Steve Tiemann

Founded

2004

Size

1,118 Acres

EDWARD "TED" AND PAT JONES-CONFLUENCE POINT STATE PARK

Late in the day, the sunlight reflects off the surface of the Missouri, as seen from the trail leading to the point where the Missouri and Mississippi Rivers merge.

Courtesy of Mark Abeln

Courtesy of Mark Abeln

The south tip of this wedge-shaped park juts into the waters where the powerful forces of the Missouri River crash into the current of the Mighty Mississippi. Looking to the south, the muddy waters of the Missouri are to the right. To the left, the waters of the Mississippi, usually more serene, reflect the blue skies. Where they meet, there is churning and a constantly reforming ripple. That ripple hints at the strength of these waters.

Walking the easy trails in the park, views of the Missouri River appear through the underbrush and woods. These sights transport visitors to the dawn of the 19th century, when the Missouri River was the highway through the territory of the Louisiana Purchase, which had doubled the size of the United States. The ghosts of fur trappers and mountain men seem to haunt the landscape. The views of the Mississippi, with white-painted tugs pushing tows of barges upstream, bring the words of Mark Twain to mind.

The history of this site and the sheer power of these rivers attract people like pilgrims. At Confluence Point, visitors can witness another natural phenomenon: the migration of millions of birds each spring and fall along the Mississippi River corridor. Sixty percent of all North American bird species migrate along the Mississippi flyway, including great blue herons, bald eagles, and many kinds of songbirds.

Until Confluence Point State Park was established in 2004, however, there was no public place to view this merging of the waters while watching the migrations of millions of birds. The acreage of Confluence Point had been plowed for crops, altering the area's ecology.

The establishment of the park, like that of so many of the state parks around St. Louis, resulted from the efforts and generosity of many St. Louisans. The Danforth Foundation of St. Louis obtained the initial 253 acres through the River Network. Later the Great Rivers Greenway (then the Metropolitan Park and Recreation District), with the Department of Natural Resources, expanded the parkland. More acres were purchased with a grant through the federal North American Wetlands Conservation Act, given to acquire, preserve, and develop wetland ecosystems for waterfowl, other migratory birds, fish, and wildlife.

The goal of this effort was to return plowed fields to wild wetlands where animals and plants flourished 200 years ago and to give visitors a window into the river confluence and its natural history. The park is named in honor of Edward "Ted" Jones (1925–1990), the managing partner of Edward D. Jones & Co., and his wife Hilda "Pat" Jones (1935–2018). The couple supported the Missouri state park system and bought land to build the Katy Trail.

Courtesy of Mark Abeln

Courtesy of Mark Abeln

Courtesy of Mark Abeln

Founded	Size	Cost
2017	More than 800 Acres	Bequest by Don Robinson

DON ROBINSON STATE PARK

Courtesy of Steve Tiemann

Glades, sandstone box canyons, cliffs, a cascading creek, forests, more than 100 kinds of mosses, and 40 species of fish are the legacy of Don Robinson—an eccentric bachelor and entrepreneur who left the park named for him to the people of Missouri. Generations of early St. Louis television-watchers felt like they knew Robinson from his low-budget commercials promoting his spot remover. Wearing funny hats in his commercials, he promoted the use of "Off" to remove stains from clothing, scuffs from woodwork, and even tar and gum from carpets. He claimed to have manufactured Off, which was sold in a tube like toothpaste, in a big dough mixer.

Robinson starting selling Off in 1952. Twelve years later, the stain remover manufacturer bought his first patch of land (320 acres) southwest of St. Louis, near Cedar Hill. Inside of four years he had acquired 843 acres, the same acreage as New York City's famous Central Park. Then he moved into a rock cabin on the land.

The land is part of the 8,000-acre LaBarque Creek watershed. The bedrock stream has pools and waterfalls along its bed. The walls of the canyon, which Robinson called the "Green Gulch," were covered in moss. Robinson called his land, one of the most diverse landscapes in eastern Missouri, "wild and wooly."

In 2012, Don Robinson passed away and left his beloved land to the Missouri Department of Natural Resources. Robinson, who lived so frugally that his cabin only had heating in the bedroom, left a fund to help maintain the state park.

Courtesy of Mark Abeln

MISSOURI DEPARTMENT OF CONSERVATION

NiNi Harris

Courtesy of Steve Tiemann

The Missouri Department of Conservation owns or leases more than 12,000 acres of land in St. Louis County, almost as much as the County Parks. The department, with the mission of protecting forests, fish, and wildlife, was only a year old when a group of friends presented it with 1,880 acres in west St. Louis County.

That was in 1938, and the department developed the acreage as Rockwoods Reservation. In 1943, another 1,388 acres were donated for Rockwoods Range. The nearly 1,000-acre Forest 44 Tract was acquired in 1990.

In North County, the Missouri Department of Conservation acquired the 2,260-acre Pelican Island, which was originally a gift of Joseph Desloge. The department leased an 812-acre site for the Saint Stanislaus Seminary Reserve and purchased the 4,300-acre Columbia Bottom property in 1997.

These Reserves, often nearby or adjacent to County Parks, municipal parks, and independent natural lands like the Tyson Research Center (the environmental research station owned by Washington University) and the Shaw Nature Reserve (a division of the Missouri Botanical Garden) are creating green corridors that preserve Ozark flora and fauna and maintain the Meramec River Valley and the Confluence of the Mississippi and Missouri Rivers.

While the Department of Conservation is protecting unique natural sites in the area, it also operates a popular resource for education, the Powder Valley Conservation Nature Center in Kirkwood, and maintains a scattering of lakes in municipal parks across the St. Louis region.

Courtesy of Steve Tiemann

Park	Founded	Size	Cost
Columbia Bottom	1997	4,451 Acres	$9.3 million
Saint Stanislaus		812 Acres Along the Missouri Riverbanks	

COLUMBIA BOTTOM CONSERVATION AREA

Brilliant yellow sunflowers, grasslands that turn brown in fall, bottomland forests, and marshy areas that dot the fields mark the floodplain in northeast St. Louis County bordering the confluence of the Missouri and Mississippi Rivers, the Columbia Bottom Conservation Area.

Nineteenth-century plat maps show a short-lived town once known as Columbia and later as St. Vrain on this river bottom in the mid-1800s. It had disappeared by 1870. The City of St. Louis bought the land in the 1940s as a possible site for a second airport. After that plan fell through, the land was leased to farmers. In 1997, the Missouri Department of Conservation acquired the expansive acreage of river bottom lands from St. Louis for $9.3 million.

This conservation area offers spectacular views of the confluence of the rivers as well as trails through a mosaic of shallow-water wetlands and grasslands while providing a natural link on the Mississippi Flyway for millions of migrating birds. Two hundred eighty-five species of birds have been recorded at Columbia Bottom Conservation Area, including rarities like the white ibis, tricolored heron, white-tailed kite, golden eagle, Swainson's hawk, prairie falcon, and northern shrike.

The Columbia Bottom Conservation Area provides an essential link in the greenway straddling the Missouri River at the confluence with the Mississippi that includes Saint Stanislaus Conservation Area, Pelican Island Natural Area, Bellefontaine Conservation Area and Fort Belle Fontaine, Sioux Passage County Parks, and the Edward "Ted" and Pat Jones-Confluence Point Missouri State Park.

Courtesy of Missouri Department of Conservation

SAINT STANISLAUS CONSERVATION AREA

The acreage was part of the retreat site for the Jesuit priests, brothers, and seminarians who were living, working, and studying at nearby Saint Stanislaus Seminary, established in 1823 by Jesuit missionaries from Belgium. A steep trail ascends Charbonier Bluff, named by the early French for the coal seam running through the rock, and offers views overlooking the Missouri River bottoms.

Courtesy of Wikimedia Commons

Park	Founded	Size	Cost
Rockwoods Reservation	1938	1880 Acres	Donated
Rockwoods Range	1943	1,453 Acres	

Courtesy of Mark Abeln

ROCKWOODS RESERVATION

Generations of St. Louisans have explored its heavily wooded hills, followed its babbling brooks, or participated in an autumn Owl Prowl in Rockwoods Reservation. At nature programs on this reservation, many children are first introduced to the concept of ecology. Along the reserve's 13 miles of enchanting trails, however, relics from its history recall that this acreage was once industrialized and barren of trees.

A lime kiln remains from a time when Glencoe Mining Company mined limestone on this site. An underground quarry called Cobbs Cavern was two stories high and larger than a football field. The company laborers logged the hills and valleys for fuel for the limestone kilns. During the Great Depression, Glencoe went bust, leaving the land bare.

In 1938, the new Missouri Department of Conservation acquired the land and began restoring nature.

ROCKWOODS RANGE

A. P. Greensfelder, a St. Louis civic leader, donated this lushly forested land punctuated by sunny glades with limestone outcroppings and desert plants. A native St. Louisan, Greensfelder (1879–1955) began working for Fruin-Colnan Contractors in 1906 and eventually served as president of the company and then chairman of the board. He volunteered with area planning commissions, promoting parks and open space.

Courtesy of Wikimedia Commons

Size

91 Acres

GATEWAY ARCH NATIONAL PARK

NiNi Harris

Courtesy of Wikimedia Commons

The Gateway Arch National Park is the only national park that preserves and interprets a setting in the heart of a city. It celebrates the heritage of this small piece of real estate—the St. Louis riverfront—that was the origin of explorations, expeditions and settlement of the American West while serving as the sole mart for these vast territories of the American West. The Gateway Arch, commemorating the 18th- and 19th-century role of the riverfront, is also an expression of the resolve and vision of its builders—the Greatest Generation. That generation survived the hardships of the Great Depression, earned victory in World War II, and then explored space, reaching the moon.

The dream of building a great riverfront monument originated in the 1930s. The design, by Finnish-American Eero Saarinen, of a 630-foot-tall, seamless stainless steel arch, was chosen in 1948. The work of building the Arch began in 1961 with the removal of 300,000 cubic feet of earth and rock for the foundation and underground museum. Workers poured 26,000 tons of concrete for the foundation of the Arch. Craftsmen set in place the first stainless steel section of the Arch on February 12, 1963.

As work progressed and the Arch was reaching for the sky, the midair construction site became more and more hazardous. At dizzying heights, whipped by wind, hardhats welded the huge triangles together with their strength and skill. With each wedge of stainless steel, each leg of the Arch grew taller and tension grew. Every St. Louisan seemed to know that if the slightest variation existed between the legs of the Arch, it could not be completed.

On October 28, 1965, activity in St. Louis came to a halt. It was the day that the keystone was to be wedged into the top of the Arch. Ten thousand St. Louisans watched from the Arch grounds, thousands more watched from their downtown office buildings and warehouses, and the rest of St. Louis watched on television as the skilled workers hoisted the keystone to the worksite—630 feet above the ground. Giant cranes forced the legs to separate slightly. To observers, it seemed that the craftsmen effortlessly slipped the keystone into the top of the stainless steel arch. The feat of engineering and construction was awe-inspiring.

The Arch was 75 feet taller than the Washington monument and 175 feet taller than the Statue of Liberty. The completed

Gateway Arch surpassed all other American monuments and rivaled the great monuments of the world.

The Arch overlooks the great Mississippi, which served as the highway to the West, and it is framed with acres of park with expansive lawns, miles of tree-lined walks and biking trails, and kidney-shaped reflecting pools that mimic the curves of the monument. A natural amphitheater is surrounded by ornamental grasses.

In recent years these grounds have been redeveloped. The underground museum has been expanded to include interactive exhibits that tell the stories of the earliest days of St. Louis as a French fur-trading post and explain the city's role as Gateway to the West.

This transformation and expansion of the parkland was fueled by voters in St. Louis City and County. At their polling places, they demonstrated their commitment when they passed a proposition in 2013 to help fund CityArchRiver, a renovation of the setting of the Gateway Arch. This is the first time in the nation's history that residents of a locality have taxed themselves to enhance a National Park.

Courtesy of Wikimedia Commons

Courtesy of Wikimedia Commons

BIBLIOGRAPHY

Annual Reports of the St. Louis Parks Department. Acreage, cost of purchase and improvements, construction and maintenance projects, and usage figures were found in these reports, 1893–1948.

Atlas of the City of St. Louis, Missouri. Philadelphia: G. M. Hopkins, C. E., 1883.

Banner, Stuart. *Legal Systems in Conflict, Property and Sovereignty in Missouri*, 1750-1860. Norman: University of Oklahoma Press, 1998.

Biggest Asset of Babler Memorial Seized in Mexico, May 18, 1938, local history file in St. Louis Room, St. Louis Public Library.

Carondelet Park tree survey completed in April 2007 by Skip Kincaid & Associates (SKA).

The Civic League of Saint Louis. *A Plan for Saint Louis, Reports of the Several Committees Appointed by the Executive Board of the Civic League to Draft a City Plan*, 1907.

Cotton, W. Philip Jr., *Clifton Heights, Preliminary Neighborhood Historical Research Report*. St. Louis: Heritage/St. Louis, 1971.

Clipping files on the St. Louis Parks, History Department, St. Louis Public Library, Main Branch.

Commonfields Map of St. Louis, redrawn by the National Park Service from the Huttawa Atlas, a compilation of 1848.

Dacus, J. A., and James W. Buel. *A Tour of St. Louis or, the Inside Life of a Great City*. St. Louis: Western Publishing Company, Jones & Griffin, 1878.

Darby, John F. *Personal Recollections of John F. Darby, Mayor of St. Louis, 1835, Sketches of Prominent People and of Events Relating to the History of St. Louis During the First Half of the Nineteenth Century*. St. Louis: G.I. Jones and Company, 1880.

Dates, Donald. Scrapbooks of Carondelet History, compiled 1945-1947.

Don Robinson interview with Anne-Marie Berger for Living St. Louis, 2009.

"Don't Despoil Lafayette Park," *St. Louis Star*, August 5, 1927, editorial, Clipping file of St. Louis Public Library.

Dry, Camille N., and Rich. J. Compton. *Pictorial St. Louis, Metropolis of the Mississippi Valley, A Topographical Survey*, 1875.

Hill, Sarah Full. *Mrs. Hill's Journal-Civil War Reminiscences*, edited by Mark M. Krug. Chicago: The Lakeside Press, 1980.

Mastodon State Historic Site The Kimmswick Bone Bed, published by the Missouri Department of Natural Resources.

Mayor's Messages. Biannual reports containing references to the parks, and sometimes reports on individual parks, prior to the 1876 separation of the City and County.

Memorial Park Outside St. Louis Will Afford Retreat from City, copyright 1936, local history file in St. Louis Room, St. Louis Public Library.

Orear, G. W. *Commercial and Architectural St. Louis*. St. Louis: Jones & Orear Publishers, 1888.

Pape, Fred W., commissioner of Parks and Recreation of the City of St. Louis. "Francis Park Destined to be One of the

Beauty Spots of St. Louis," *City Beautiful*, April 1930.

Park report dated November 1874 included in Mayor's Message of January 1875.

The Past in Our Presence: Historic Buildings in St. Louis County. St. Louis County, Missouri, 1996.

Pitzman, Julius. *Pitzman's New Atlas of the City and County of Saint Louis Missouri*. Philadelphia: A. B. Holcombe & Co., 1878.

Reavis, L. U. *Saint Louis: The Future Great City of the World*. St. Louis: Gray, Baker & Co., 1875.

St. Louis Area Cemeteries, compiled by the Microfilm Department and the History and Genealogy Departments of St. Louis Public Library, April 2005.

Saint Louis Illustrated: Her Public Buildings, Churches, Press, Parks, Gardens, People, Schools, Railroads, Commerce, Manufactories, Etc. St. Louis: Will Conklin, 1876.

St. Louis Globe-Democrat, July 25, 1934, local history file in St. Louis Room, St. Louis Public Library.

Saint Louis Post-Dispatch, March 3, 1931, "Electrocuted while Watching Hotel Fire," p. 3A.

Saint Louis Post-Dispatch, July 24, 1959, "Reliving the Gay Old Days at Lincoln Beach," by Dickson Terry, p. 3D.

Saint Louis Post-Dispatch, January 20, 1974, "Planned Park Aimed at Urban Outdoorsman," by Eric L Zoeckler, p. 3B.

Saint Louis Post-Dispatch, September 8, 1975, "Bond Sets Up Meramec River Area," by Fred W. Lindeck, p. 1A.

Saint Louis Post-Dispatch, August 8, 1978.

Saint Louis Post-Dispatch, August 1, 1978, "Meramec Trade-off Is Undisputed," by Jeff Gelles, p. 3B.

Saint Louis Post-Dispatch, November 6, 1979, "Castlewood: New Park in County," by Dick Richmond, p. 1D.

Saint Louis Post-Dispatch, August 21, 1985, "Mastodon State Park to Get Museum," by Victor Volland, p. 3A.

Saint Louis Post-Dispatch, November 7, 1985, "Ground Break Is Set for Mastodon Museum," p. 3A.

Saint Louis Post-Dispatch, June 28, 1989, "Model of Giant Skeleton Looms Large in Park," by Patricia Rice, p. 1F.

Saint Louis Post-Dispatch, "State Plans to Restore Confluence Point Park as Wetlands," by Sara Shipley, January 7, 2003, p. 1B

Saint Louis Post-Dispatch, "Where the Waters Meet," May 2, 2004, by Valerie Schremp, p. C1.

Saint Louis Post-Dispatch, "Missouri Gets Park Site Where Rivers Meet," by William Allen, February 8, 2007.

Scharf, J. Thomas. *History of St. Louis City and County, from the Earliest Periods to the Present Day*. Philadelphia: Louis H. Everts & Co., 1883.

Souvenir of Carondelet, a promotional booklet published in the early 1890s.

Watchman Advocate, November 29, 1935, "Parks and River Projects in County and Vicinity Costing Millions Under Construction."

Wells, Rolla. *Episodes of My Life*. St. Louis, 1933.

World's Largest Open Air Swimming Pool Draws Half Million, *WPA Allots Funds for Babler Park Work*, August 28, 1939, local history file in St. Louis Room, St. Louis Public Library. *Forward St. Louis*, May 4, 1914.

Courtesy of Steve Tiemann

INDEX OF FEATURED PARKS

ABOUT THE PHOTOGRAPHERS

Mark Abeln is a native of St. Louis and attended college at Caltech, in Pasadena, California. Mark started taking photography seriously after he took disappointing photos of an important subject. He spent the next years learning the art of photography, and his photos can now be found in numerous publications as well as on his website, Rome of the West.

Steve Tiemann graduated from McCluer High School and went on to obtain his forestry degree from the University of Missouri at Columbia. Steve has enjoyed his career with the St. Louis County Park Rangers for nearly 30 years and always has a camera at hand to capture those magic moments in the beautiful outdoors.

A St. Louis photo-documenter and owner of St. Louis City Talk, **Mark Groth** was born in Fort Knox, Kentucky; raised in Belleville, Illinois; and has lived in six different neighborhoods in St. Louis since 1994. See neighborhood, park, library tours, and much more at stlouiscitytalk.com